LOST TREASURES
ON THE OLD SPANISH TRAIL

George A. Thompson

WESTERN EPICS
254 South Main
Salt Lake City, Utah 84101

ISBN: 0-914740-31-8

"There is something in a treasure that fastens upon a man's mind. He will pray and blaspheme and still persevere, and will curse the day he heard of it, and will let his last hour come upon him unawares, still believing that he missed it by only a foot. He will see it every time he closes his eyes. He will never forget it until he is dead, and perhaps not even then. There is no getting away from a treasure that once fastens itself upon your mind."

—Conrad, Nostromo

PREFACE

The Old Spanish Trail! From the arrival of the first Americans in the west it has been a mystery, like a giant jig-saw puzzle with some of the pieces missing. Until recently, about all we knew for sure was that it existed, but we didn't know who first used it, or when. But newly discovered documents and journals have added a few more pieces to the puzzle, so that now we can set the record straight and tell its story as it really is. Some historians have claimed the old trail is of recent origin, first used by Mexican merchants and later by American fur trappers, who came to the Great Basin after Mexican independence from Spain in 1821. Nothing could be further from the truth, for the old trail is an ancient one, followed by the first conquistadores. It was named by Don Antonio Espejo in 1580, but it was an old trail even then.

In the days of Cortez the old trail started at Mexico City, but by the time of Coronado its trail-head was located as far north as Compostela and even Culiacan. It would soon be pushed even further northward, to El Paso del Norte. In 1598 Juan de Onate established its most northerly outpost at Santa Fe and by the mid-1600s its many forks extended from Colorado and Utah far into Wyoming, Idaho and Nevada. Those are facts, with enough evidence to convince any open-minded person. There is no doubt that Spanish adventurers, miners, slavers and priests travelled the old trail to nearly every desert canyon and snowy peak between the Rockies and the Sierras while the Pilgrim Fathers were still exploring the rocky coast of New England.

The Old Spanish Trail had but one purpose, to serve as a roadway to the legendary land of Cibola and the treasures of gold and silver waiting to be found there. It wasn't built for commerce or to civilize the Indians, or even to convert them to Christianity. Its only purpose was Cibola and gold, and those who followed it were treasure hunters first and missionaries afterwards. And contrary to popular belief, Cortez wasn't the first treasure hunter, only one of the most successful, and Cibola wasn't invented during the time of Coronado, it was a legend old even in the time of Columbus. While countless thousands were following the old trail north in search of treasure, the dream of Cibola died with the Coronado expedition on the barren plains of Kansas. But the death of Cibola gave birth to an even greater dream, the quest for the mysterious lake of Copalla and the fabled land of Teguayo. It was the search for Teguayo, not Cibola, that opened the entire Great Basin to exploration.

From the time of Captain-General Francisco Coronado in 1540 to that of Father Geronimo Salmeron a century later, every explorer sought the great lake which the Indians called Copalla and the rich mines in the mountains beyond, in the land they called Teguayo. By the middle of the seventeenth century, Spanish miners had found many of the Indian's mines and claimed them as their own, sentencing their former owners to forced labor in them. After the "northern mystery" was solved, that rich region underwent many name changes, from Cibola to Teguayo, and later from Timpanocutzis to Utah Valley. But the Old Spanish Trail didn't end even there, for another 100 years Spanish miners and Mexican slavers followed it even further north, to rich mines in the Uinta and Wind River mountains, and even beyond.

All across the Great Basin and the mountain ranges which surround it, Spanish miners worked mines of gold and silver with Indian slave labor, while Jesuit Priests built missions where the native's life was no less harsh than it was in the mines. Those missions were not the splendid churches we usually associate with the southwest, but were more often visitas, crude places built of adobe or rubble-stone, boasting little more than a rough plank altar. In every western state the first French and English trappers, and later the Mountain Men and pioneers found long abandoned Spanish mines and the crumbling ruins of Jesuit missions. Proof of their antiquity can be seen in the names, dates and Catholic crosses carved on ancient trees or inscribed onto ledge rock along the old trails leading to them. Although some of the dates are dim and the names are now unknown, the fact that they are there can't be denied, and they were old when the earliest

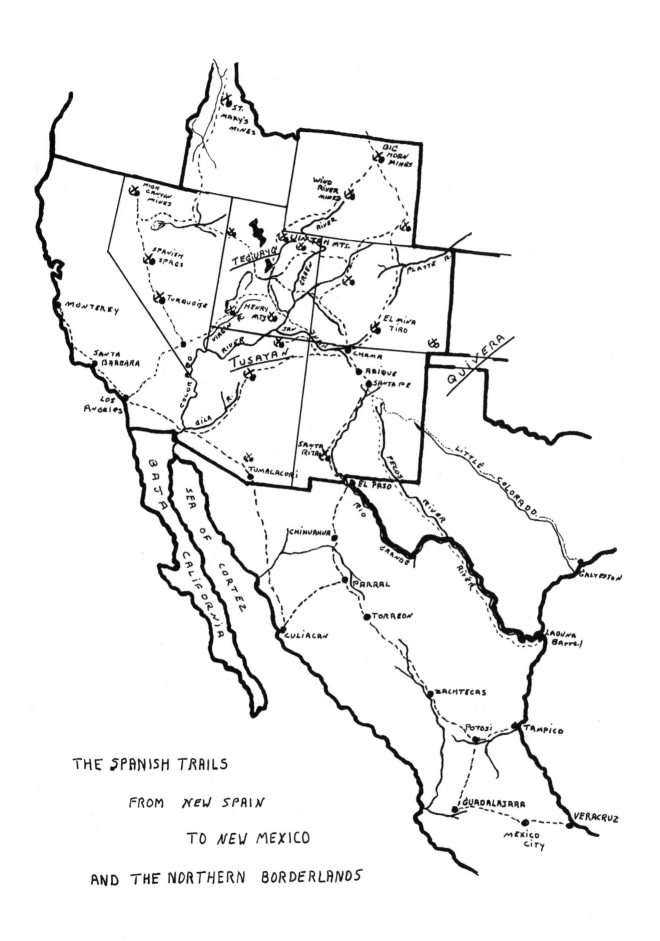

THE SPANISH TRAILS

FROM NEW SPAIN

TO NEW MEXICO

AND THE NORTHERN BORDERLANDS

explorers first saw them.

There isn't an Indian nation that doesn't have legends or traditions of forced labor at Spanish mines or missions. One need only research ancient Spanish civil or church records to learn the extent of slavery, and the terrible toll it took on the Indians. Nearly every journal left by the explorers of the mountain west contain references to the Spanish slave trade, and of slave markets at places like Taos and Santa Fe. Official Spanish documents located at the archives at Santa Fe, Mexico City and Seville reveal that ten billion dollars in gold and silver was shipped to Spain from the mines of the new world, during which time the Indian population was decimated by one-half. It is a fact that almost every ounce of precious metal sent to the Royal Court came from Spanish mines worked by Indian slaves.

The enslavement of the Indians finally led to revolts which drove the Spaniards from their mines, and resulted in the expulsion of the Jesuit Order from their mountain missions. It took nearly two decades before Spanish soldiers could force their way back into the mountains. During that time most of their mines had been concealed and their missions destroyed. Fabulously rich mines such as the famed Josephine de Martinique, El Mina del Tiro and the Lost Mine Of The Yutahs were never found, while mysterious maps and cryptic waybills were left to lead the way to cached mission treasures. It was a time when legends were born, and most of them were true.

After the Spaniards were driven from the land and the Americans replaced the Mexicans, pioneers and settlers found many of the old mines and missions, but even more were never found. The Spanish conquistadores had shipped more gold and silver to Spain than was then known in the entire world, but still more was left behind, most of it hidden in mines concealed during the Indian revolt or buried by Jesuit Priests when they were arrested and expelled from their missions. For every old mine or mission found, many more are still lost. The greatest treasures of all still remain to be found.

And what of the Old Spanish Trail? Traces of it can still be found at places like the Sinbad Desert and Canyonlands, where it was worn deeply into soft sandstone rock by the passing of countless pack trains, heavily laden with plundered treasure. It can be followed from the Spanish Bottoms on the Colorado River, where hand-cut steps can still be seen, to the San Rafael River, where ancient dates and Catholic crosses are cut into ledge rock. Traces of it remain from the Wasatch Mountains to Monument Valley, and across the deserts of New Mexico to the Texas gulf coast, where Spanish galleons waited to carry fortunes in gold and silver to the king's coffers at Seville and Madrid. The Old Spanish Trail is real. It can still be seen, from the deserts of Sonora to the mountains of Wyoming. And the fabulous lost mines and forgotten missions along its lonely miles are real too, but their lost treasures are harder to find. With a lot of research and a little luck, the following pages could be your waybill to the lost treasures of the Old Spanish Trail!

CHAPTER ONE

THE LEGEND OF CIBOLA

"History knows of no man who ever did the like."

—Epitaph of Christopher Columbus
Cathedral of Seville, Spain

In the time of Columbus it was well known that in about the year 750 AD, a Bishop of Lisbon had sailed into the unknown western sea and reached a land where there were seven cities very rich in gold. Even at that early date some called them the Seven Cities of Cibola. Nearly a half-century before the historic first voyage of Columbus, Gregorio Garcia recorded in his epic history, Origen de los Indios, that in the year 1448, Portuguese sailors had sailed to an island where seven cities of gold were discovered. In 1482 Cibola was shown on the latest maps prepared by Graciosus Benincasa. He placed that fabled land on the Island of Antilia, somewhere across the unknown western sea near the very edge of the world.

The adventures of Marco Polo had only recently become known, including the account of his overland journey to China and the Island of Cipango (Japan), and of the fabulous treasures he found there. Spanish adventurers, then the world's greatest sailors, remembered the ancient legend of the seven cities, which told of a rich land sometimes called Cibola and sometimes called Antilia, and in their minds Marco Polo's Cipango and the treasure island of Antilia became one and the same. The possibilities of more gold than the world had ever known didn't go unnoticed at the Royal Court of Spain's King Ferdinand V and Queen Isabella. If Cibola was an island, why not sail westward to it and avoid the five-year overland journey it had taken Marco Polo to reach it? And so the dream of Cibola was born anew.

The first treasure hunter to seek Cibola was Cristobal Colon, the man now remembered as Christopher Columbus. Although others sought to be first, circumstances dictated that Columbus would be the first to sail into the unknown in the service of his king. Contrary to what some have said, his first goal was gold, not Christianity or the discovery of new lands. He was looking for Cibola and nothing else. As early as 1490 Columbus had written: "Gold is most excellent, of gold is treasure made, with gold the man who possesses it does all that he desires in the world, and may even send souls to paradise!" The official agreement made on April 17th, 1492, between Columbus and the Royal Court stated in part, "That all and whatever merchandise, whether it be pearls, precious stones, gold, silver, spices and other things, however it might be discovered, acquired or obtained, he may take for himself the tenth part of all of them, and do with it as he will, the other nine parts remaining for His Highness."

The hardships of that historic voyage of 1492 need not be repeated here, suffice it to say that upon his return to Spain, Columbus received a magnificent reception, honors and a title in return for his discovery "of a land fair and rich for planting, for building towns and villages, and as much gold as His Highness may need, spices and cotton and a thousand other precious things." And if anyone doubted his claims, he had nuggets of the purest gold to show them! In all Columbus made four voyages to the new world, in 1492, 1493, 1498 and 1502. He discovered the Bahamas, Cuba, Haiti, Puerto Rico, Jamaica, and Trinidad. Later he explored the coast of America north from Honduras to Yucatan, Nicaragua, Costa Rica, Panama and "other places in the land of Montezuma," now Mexico. His exact landing sites and places of exploration can't be located precisely because of the inaccurate maps of that period. But if we could retrace the last journey of Columbus, we might be able to locate what no doubt became America's first lost mine.

In 1503 Columbus sent a report from the Indies to his King: "On the 6th day of February, while it rained continually, I sent 70 men inland for five leagues, where they found many mines of gold.

The Indians brought them to a very high mountain where they showed them places as far as the eye could see, saying that in every part there was gold enough, and towards the west the mines stretched for twenty days, where in only ten days a man alone might gather a fanega (bushel) of gold!" Columbus had neither the manpower or supplies to seek those mines, however, in 1504 he returned to Spain to organize a better prepared expedition. Unfortunately, he died before he could return to the new world. Where are his mines of gold today?

Note that upon arrival of Columbus and the very first European explorers of record in the new world, native Indians showed them places where they already had mines of gold and silver. Mining was not something the Indians learned from the Spaniards as some suppose, but something they had already engaged in for centuries. But their interest in the precious metals was not to gain wealth, but rather for personal adornment, and as a trade item. Gold, native silver, and to a lesser degree, copper, were mallable metals, easily melted or hammered into desired shapes and forms, or fashioned into bracelets and other ornaments. Indians who had such metals or the trinkets made from them, could trade for sea shells, brightly colored feathers and other desirable things which other tribes had. Gold especially was so soft that it could be hammered into thin sheets to cover temple walls, or when melted, cast into many forms, such as the idols which represented their gods.

During recent times archaeologists using modern carbon-14 and potassium-argon dating methods have proven that the Incas were mining gold as early as 800 BC, and that by the time of Columbus they were recovering as much as twenty tons of the precious metal every year. The Aztecs of Mexico had accumulated even greater wealth by the same time. The degree of Indian civilization north of Mexico had not developed as highly as that of the Inca or Aztec nations, nevertheless, the native inhabitants of our present western states were not unaware of the trade value of gold, silver and turquoise, and had mines of their own almost as early as did those nations further south.

We now know that Indians worked the ancient copper mines at Santa Rita, New Mexico, as early as 1200 AD. As recently as 1965 a prehistoric Indian cache was found when the already deep mine shafts there broke into the long sealed workings of an Indian mine. In the cache were 1,200 turquoise beads and 240 pendants, as well as many delicately carved birds and frogs. Many ancient stone hammers and picks were also found at the cache site. Artifacts of the Anasazi found at the "Moqui" ruins where they once lived reveal that they had also developed metalurgy to some degree and were very fond of metal ornaments, for among the ruins have been found small copper bells, pendants and trinkets of turquoise. Among the Hohokam ruins of the Gila River in Arizona, researchers have found many small copper bells, similar to sleigh bells in size, but pear shaped.

The extent of Indian mining during the pre-Spanish period has been proven by many competent authorities, well known archaeologist F.H. Roberts among them. He has dated Indian turquoise mines twelve centuries before arrival of the Spaniards. He discovered that some of their more sophisticated mines had deep shafts and tunnels, as well as stopes (rooms) so large they had to leave pillars of rock as much as twenty feet thick to support them. When the first Americans arrived in the intermountain west they first believed that many of the Indian mines they found were of Spanish origin because they didn't believe Indians were capable of excavating such extensive diggings.

Literally thousands of Indian mines, many of them hundreds of feet deep, have been found, with shafts dug in a zig-zag manner to facilitate climbing in and out of them. When they were reopened by American miners, only Indian tools were found, such as shaped stone hammers and mauls. Picks were sharp, narrow instruments made from the hardest stone, while many were fashioned from deer and elk antlers. Drills were made from a sharp edged stone fastened into the end of a split hardwood stick and wrapped with wet leather, which shrunk as it dried. Those drills were used by rolling them between the hands while the weight of the body on the opposite end of the stick pressed the sharpened stone point against the ore being drilled. Several such drills have been found in the old Indian mines at Grand Gulch, Utah.

One of the earliest and most amazing finds of Indian metalurgy was reported by Dorantes de Carranza, a Spanish sailor shipwrecked with Cabeza de Vaca and others on the gulf coast of

Florida in 1527. For eight years Dorantes and his companions wandered across the southwest before reaching Culiacan on the coast of Mexico. During their wanderings they "found many signs of Copper, gold and other metals," and at a place now believed to have been in the Davis Mountains of Texas, Dorantes was given "a small copper bell or rattle, with a face etched on it," which the Indians told him "came from the north where the bell was cast." Dorantes and his three companions were the first Spaniards the Indians had ever seen, the first white men to cross the southwest. The bell given to them was not of European manufacture, but was definitely of Indian origin, proof positive that the Indians of the north were familiar not only with mining ores, but also with crude smelting, metalurgy and casting metals.

The wealth of the Indies reported by Columbus created the greatest possible excitement at the Court of Ferdinand and Isabella. Soon other nations, including France, Britain and Portugal were readying their own fleets to explore and claim their share of the treasures to be found there. It became imperative that Spanish sailors should lose no time in exploring and claiming the newfound El Dorado for His Most Catholic Majesty, as well as for His Holiness, the Pope of Rome. At that time the Royal Court of Spain was the symbolic and visual representative of papal authority throughout the Christian world, therefore, by an "Apostalic Bull" decreed by Pope Alexander VI himself, "so that the heathen Indians of the new world might be converted to the faith, all of the lands now known or yet to be discovered" were to be divided between the kings of Spain and Portugal. Because of Spain's unmatched sea power as well as the zeal of its monarchs, most of the gold and glory of the new world was claimed by its conquistadores.

The Spanish king interpreted the Pope's order as a legitimate title to all lands discovered by his subjects, by whatever means. All that was needed to claim title to a whole new country was a brief ships landing, or even a glimpse of a shoreline. In short order Spain claimed all of America's Atlantic coast from Florida to Labrador, and everything west of the gulf coast to the Pacific, even though the Pacific, then the South Sea, hadn't even been discovered. Within only a few more years they claimed all of the Pacific coast from Panama to the icy shores of Alaska. The lands claimed by Portugal were those chiefly in South America, particularly in the Amazon River basin.

Not to be overlooked was another prize then sought with almost as much fervor and zeal as was Cibola itself, the legendary Straits of Anian. It had long been believed that somewhere north of Mexico, a narrow water passage connected the Atlantic and Pacific Oceans, what a century later the British sought as the Northwest Passage. The English navigator, Sir Francis Drake, described it as being somewhere north of California. There was no doubt in the minds of Spanish sailors that such a passage existed, for as early as 1500, Gaspar Cartereal, a Portuguese, claimed he had actually sailed to Asia through the narrow waterway, while one Father Grinaldi said he too had sailed "through Anian, no more than 10 or 12 leagues wide," from China to Grand Tartary.

That there was exploration of the Atlantic coast at such an early date is proven by a map made in 1499 and now in possession of The Royal Geographic Society at London, which clearly depicts the coast of New England as it was explored by John Lloyd, "John the Skilful," in 1475, seventeen years before the first voyage of Columbus. Of equal interest is a world globe made in 1536 which shows the New England area and the Hudson River, 110 years before Henry Hudson officially discovered it. The Spanish Crown knew that if the long sought after Straits of Anian could be found, they would open a shorter route to the markets of Asia, but even more important, they would open a whole new continent for conquest, and somewhere in its vast regions was Cibola, the greatest treasure of them all. And for the Pope, there would be vast new lands peopled by native Indians, all with souls to be saved.

Although a legend almost as old as Cibola itself, Spain spent fortunes seeking the Straits of Anian. One of their most daring attempts was the expedition of Giacomo Gastaloi in 1562. The straits were later shown on a map recorded in Il Diregno del Discaperto della Nova Franza, drawn by Balognino Zoltieri in 1556. Even as late as 1600 one Juan de Fuca claimed their discovery and drew them on his charts as Fretum Anium. The real importance of the search for the legendary straits to the historian-treasure hunter was the extensive exploration for them, both by sea and by land. The search was no less important than the search for Cibola in exploring the new world. Spanish ships sailed up the Pacific coast as far as Alaska seeking their western opening, while uncounted overland expeditions marched north from Mexico looking for them, and at the same time exploring the American West from the Rio Grande to the Canadian Rockies.

Many of those now forgotten explorers were among the first Europeans to penetrate the western wilderness. Although who they were may never be known, we do know that they trod much of the intermountain west hundreds of years before much later but better authenicated explorations were made. The proof of their passing has been pre-served to the present in the trails, stone ruins, inscribed dates and other physical evidence they left behind. And every returning expedition brought back still more stories that they had nearly reached Cibola itself, that just beyond the northern mountains they had found old trails and signs which would lead to the fabled cities of gold, where streets were paved with silver and everyone lived in regal splendor. Each time the story was repeated the seven cities became a little larger, and the treasures there a little richer. Those forgotten frontiersmen were the first to blaze the long trail northward which in time would become known as the Old Spanish Trail. Meanwhile the golden dreams were coming true for conquistadores like Balboa, Cortez and Pizarro.

CHAPTER TWO

OF GODS, MEN AND SLAVES

"The heroic actions and deeds that we accomplished when we won New Spain in the company of the daring Captain Cortez I myself saw. I have no other wealth to leave my children except this true and remarkable story."

— Bernal Del Castillo

Vasco Nunez de Balboa was numbered among the first Spanish treasure hunters. It was in 1513 that he discovered the "South Sea," the Pacific Ocean, and claimed all of the land of Castilla del Oro for Spain. He discovered the wealth of the Indies to be greater than even that of the Spanish Crown, but the hardships his men suffered getting those riches for the king were terrible, and in a letter written to His Majesty on January 20th, 1513, he told how food was more important to them than gold. "I have taken care that everything obtained has been properly divided, the gold and the pearls, but we have valued food more than the gold, for we have more gold than health, and I have searched in many directions, desirous more to find a sack of corn than a bag of gold."

Like Columbus before him, Balboa discovered Indian mines which had been worked for centuries. He was among the first to describe Indian mining methods. "The Indians collect the gold without any trouble, after the river beds are laid bare. They also wait until the hills are dry and then set fire to them, where they gather great quantities of beautiful grains of gold. They bring it in to be melted, to the Indian they call Davaive, who has a great place for melting it in his house, and where he has a hundred men continually working at the gold." It is very clear that even the earliest Spanish explorers discovered that the Indians were excellent miners and even had places where they worked the gold. Balboa's letter and the hoard of treasure he sent to King Ferdinand quickly encouraged even better equipped treasure hunts. In 1518, Don Juan de Grijalva was dispatched to the gulf coast to investigate stories of gold and gems to be found there. Grijalva did find treasures wonderful to behold, but his expedition was destined to be overshadowed by the fantastic odyssey of Cortez only a year later.

Hernando Cortez was born in 1485, and at age 17 became a soldier for the king. By 1504 he had made his way to Hispanola, now Haiti, where his uncle was the governor. His uncle offered young Cortez a plantation, to which Cortez replied, "I came to get gold, not to till the soil like a peasant!" Cortez did accept a large plantation, however, which soon made him rich. In 1519 he was commissioned Captain-General of the Indies by his uncle. With some 550 men, but only 16 horses and 14 cannons, Cortez sailed westward to explore the Gulf Coast. On April 21st, 1519, he landed near where Columbus had sailed a generation earlier. From there he began the conquest of Mexico, burning his ships behind him so that his frightened men could not desert him.

Indian runners quickly informed Emperor Montezuma of the ship's landing, and the Emperor, with hope of bribing the Spaniards not to march on Mexico City, sent a chief with more than one hundred Indians bearing gifts for Cortez. "The first was a great disk six feet high, representing the sun, with many designs on it, the whole of pure gold. The next was an even larger disk of pure silver, which represented the moon. They then gave us golden ducks, monkeys, tigers, deer and lions, all beautifully worked and natural looking, also many precious necklaces, golden scepters, arm and leg bands and head bands, all of the finest gold, and then taking one of our helmets, they filled it with gold also." But instead of appeasing Cortez, the almost unbelievable gifts only whetted his appetite for more. Taking 400 of his best men, armed with deadly harquebus firearms, Cortez faced the Emperor Montezuma's forces of tens of thousands of well disciplined fighters. If it had not been for the Aztec God Quetzalcoatl, the Spanish invaders would have been slaughtered.

To the Aztecs, Quetzalcoatl was a fair skinned

God of peace, who according to legend had once lived among them. He taught them not only the ways of peace and happiness, but also how to cast metals, how to record the calculations of the Toltec calendar and many other useful things. But his power was not as great as their God of War, so he was forced to leave his people. Quetzalcoatl disappeared into the east, but he promised that one day he would return to live among them again and teach them the ways of peace. According to the legend, Quetzalcoatl said, "When the time has come, I will return to your midst, from the eastern sea, accompanied by white and bearded men."

When Montezuma received the news that a fair-skinned, God-like figure had arrived from the east in a great sailing ship, he believed that Quetzalcoatl had returned as promised. Although many of his closest advisors doubted that Cortez was really a God, Montezuma allowed his small army to march inland, where after an 83 day forced march between the 18,000 foot volcanic peaks named Popocatepetl and Citlalteptl they arrived at the island city of Tenochtitlan, Mexico City, where they looked upon the palace of the Emperor. When Cortez demonstrated to Montezuma that simply by pointing his harquebus rifle at one of his bodyguards, the guard would be killed, and that his horses, animals which the terrified Indians had never seen, could catch anyone he ordered them to, Montezuma accepted him as Quetzalcoatl, saying, "You must be a God!"

At Mexico City Cortez was astounded by the wealth of the Aztecs. For centuries Indians from distant provinces in the north had paid the Emperor tribute in gold and silver, so that by the arrival of Cortez, their storehouses were filled with treasure and more was being received at the rate of two tons each year. Temples were heavily plated with gold, while almost every native appeared to wear ornaments of precious metals and gemstones. Cortez was presented with gifts he could never have imagined existed, gold necklaces and jewelry, a turquoise face mask, woven gold textiles, and most impressive of all, disks of hammered gold and silver the size of cart wheels. When he saw how little value the Indians placed on their fabulous treasures, Cortez took Montezuma prisoner and held him for ransom. Within only a few days the citizens of Mexico City filled a room seventeen by

twenty-two feet in size with gold for their Emperor's release. But when Cortez saw how easily the huge ransom had been collected, he refused to release Montezuma.

The Spaniards were appalled at the human sacrifices made daily by the Aztecs, and were horrified by an estimated 100,000 human skulls they were shown. "Opening up the human breasts, they pulled the still beating heart out and offered them on their heinous altars. Then, believing they had made a ritual sacrifice to their heathen Gods, they ate the flesh of their victims." Enraged at the Indian's barbarism, Cortez ordered their idols destroyed, then fearing an attack, he had 3,000 Indians slaughtered. The Indians revolted, and in a terrible battle drove the Spaniards from the city, losing additional thousands of warriors, but inflicting heavy losses on the Spaniards. Forty-five of his already small army had been killed while 60 more were badly wounded. Cortez had the bodies of his dead soldiers secretly buried so that the Indians wouldn't know that Gods could be killed. Cortez and his men had the great advantage of armor, including metal helmets, jackets of mail and heavy iron or leather shields. A priest described the advantage of armor. "A soldier, well armored and mounted on an armored horse is like a moving fortress. The soldiers have become most dextrous in making armor for their horses, using a thickness of two bull hides, through which arrows cannot penetrate. Because of the weight of the armor, the horse is not used until the moment of battle. The point of danger lies in the possibility of an Indian throwing himself under the horse to sever its tendons. A soldier heavily laden with armor, once fallen from the horse, is at the mercy of savages who carry war clubs, lances and bows with arrows."

The battle to regain Mexico City was a terrible one, which according to Cortez, resulted in the deaths of nearly 100,000 Indians. He wrote: "Because I feared the enemy was so compact that my men might be crushed by their great numbers, I ordered my soldiers to do damage with our field pieces. No understanding can conceive how they endured it. An infinite number of men, women and children kept coming towards us, who in their haste pushed one another into the water and were drowned amidst their multitude of dead. It appears they perished there to the number of more than 50,000. The slaughter done that day on land numbered more than 40,000 men, and it was not possible to prevent the massacre of 15,000 more, until we could no longer endure the stench of the dead, who had lain for days on the streets."

Cortez and his soldiers finally fought their way back into the city on August 13th, 1521, but by then Montezuma was dead, stoned to death by his own people, and most of his fabulous treasure had been hidden. It has never been found, but Aztec legend tells that the Emperor's servant, Tlahuicle, at Montezuma's order, took the vast treasure hundreds of miles to the north to their ancestral home where much of it had come from, and where it was hidden in a great cavern. Today many believe that Montezuma's treasure is hidden in the depths of White Mountain, near present day Kanab, Utah, but more about that later.

At Mexico City Cortez found hoards of treasure which had been hidden by its citizens, and also recovered part of Montezuma's ransom, which had been thrown into the lake when his soldiers were forced from the city. Only a small part of the treasure was recovered, but still it was a fabulous fortune. Recovered were "150,000 castellanos of gold, 88,000 pesos in gold bars, thousands of gold plates and a mass of jewels." From one sealed treasure room found by his soldiers, Cortez took "gold worth more than 600,000 ducats, which we melted into bars three fingers wide." During the next two years Cortez sent ten tons of gold to Spain as the King's Quinto, his one-fifth share, more than all of the nations of Europe except Spain then possessed!

In a letter to the king, Cortez described some of the Royal Fifth. "Of all the gold smelted, one-fifth was put aside for the Royal Treasury, as well as jewels, 33,000 ounces of gold in ingots and 60,000 ounces in gold castellanos. I also sent a field piece made entirely of silver, which cost me in metal working alone some 35,000 ounces of gold This I sent as well as certain gold and silver ornaments, jewels and gems." Of the richness of the land, Viceroy Marques de Montesclaras later wrote, "Truly the land is overflowing with wealth, so that it is deemed easier and cheaper to arm men and to shoe horses with silver than it is with iron!"

The earliest explorers quickly learned that the new world was a virtual treasure house of precious metals and gem stones, but they were restricted from working the mines where the treasures came from by their sheer lack of numbers. Only a few hundred Spaniards arrived with each galleon, and their numbers were decimated by disease and warfare with the Indians who greatly outnumbered them. Of 1,300 Spanish soldiers who had been sent to the new world by then, Indians had killed 862. Many had been eaten by cannibal tribes along the Mexican coast. Balboa had described the state of affairs to the king. "Two days journey from here there is very beautiful country, inhabited by a very evil race, who eat as many of our men as they can get. They have no chief and are the lords of the mines, which are the richest in the world. These Indians have deserved death a thousand times over, for they are a very evil race who have killed many of our Christians. I would not make slaves of so bad a people, but would order them to be destroyed, both old and young, so that no memory of them might remain!"

As early as 1495 Columbus had solved the problem of the lack of Spanish manpower to work in the mines or at plantations by a system called Encomienda, which in effect assigned Indians to provide labor and tribute to a Spanish overlord in order to receive Christian instructions from him, but it became just another name for slavery. After an uprising, Columbus imposed a tribute on the Indians. He taxed each "a hawksbill of gold or an arroba (25 pounds) of cotton every three months." He then assigned their already cultivated lands to the Spaniards, and each allotment included the forced labor of its former owner. In 1502 the king legalized the Encomienda, and except for a short period from 1542 to 1545 it remained the law of the Indies for 300 years. By 1520 the king had also authorized the branding of slaves, but stipulated that they should not be branded on the face! It was the Encomienda system, slavery, that made possible the legal looting of the wealth of the Americas, for Indians were soon being forced to work in mines or on rancherias under the most terrible conditions.

Each grant of land given by the king included a specified number of Indians, each of whom was expected to pay tribute. His Royal Orders read: "Also, because in order to secure gold and do the other tasks that I am ordering done, it will be necessary to employ the service of Indians, and you are to compel them to work in the affairs of our service." If the Indians could not pay their assessed tribute, they could work their tax out as vassals. Since they couldn't pay the tribute, there became no real distinction between the Encomienda and actual slavery.

It probably never occurred to the king that New Spain was anything except his personal property, existing for the sole purpose of enriching his royal treasury. Therefore, if it was necessary for the Indians to perform the heavy work at the mines and ranches, so be it. Indians were considered equal only to stock animals, to be disposed of at the will of the landlord or transferred on sale of the land to a new owner. Little wonder that by the end of the third century of Spanish occupation, the Indian population of the Americas had been reduced to one-half its former number!

CHAPTER THREE

The Encomienda

"You are already taking our land away from us. If we show you where the yellow stones are, you will drive us away or kill us."

—Lament of the Indian

Despite the fact that Pope Alexander himself had directed that the Indians be treated fairly, and should even be paid for their labor, all with the hope of converting them to Christianity, gold proved to be more important than God to the Spanish Crown. Not only did King Ferdinand authorize the Encomienda, in 1519 the newly crowned monarch King Charles I directed that under certain conditions wars could be waged against the Indians to enslave them. The Royal Decree, written by Dr. Gines de Sepulveda, allowed the Indians to be captured, enslaved or even killed if necessary under four different circumstances. "(1) The gravity of their crimes, particularly idolatry or sins against nature. (2) The rudeness of their minds, barbarous by nature. (3) For the sake of the faith, since their subjugation will make it more convenient to teach them the faith. (4) Because they do harm to each other, killing and sometimes eating each other." Thus started the system that in 300 years reduced the Indians from an estimated five million to less than half that number, and made slavery legal from Mexico to the northern Rockies. Since the Indians were not Christians, but were "barbarous by nature," wars waged to enslave them were perfectly legal.

Amazingly, before warfare could be directed against the Indians, the military commander was required to read a prepared statement to them, even though its complex and legal language was entirely unintelligible to the Indians. Called the Requerimiento, it informed the Indians that if they resisted subjugation and enslavement, any injuries or death they might sustain would be their fault, not the Spaniards. It stated in part: "I certify that with the help of God we shall make war against you in all ways and manners that we can, and shall subject you to the yoke of obedience to the Church. We shall take your wives and children and shall make slaves of them, and we shall take away your goods and shall do you all the harm and damage that we can, as vassals who do not obey their lord, and that the death and losses which shall accrue from this are your fault and not that of His Highness." It was gentlemanly and very correct, but the poor Indian never understood a word of it.

Letters written to Viceroy Velasco by his advisor, Alfonso Messia, and also by Don Francisco de Toledo described the Encomienda and the terrible toll it took on the Indians. "As lands are allotted to the conquerors, forced labor is soon found necessary, nor are the Priests and Monks always adverse to it. It amounts to recruiting Indians for compulsory labor for work defined as being in the public interest, including tilling the soil and mining. Some 2,200 Indians are taken to the mines of Potosi each year, and with their wives and children they constitute some 7,000 souls. Of that number, no more than 2,000 ever return alive, the rest die at Potosi." There have been many armchair historians who have written that Indians were never made to work in Spanish mines, but since the conquistadores had been given express permission by the king to enslave the Indians, it is difficult to understand why those writers have said they did not, just as one might wonder why they also deny that Spaniards worked mines of gold and silver, when in their own records the Spaniards themselves said that they did.

One Solarzano Pereira described working conditions in the Spanish mines. "And the work is so excessive at that, working twelve hours a day, going down into the mines for 400, and at times 700 feet, down to where night is perpetual, for it is always necessary to work by candlelight, the air thick and ill-smelling, being enclosed in the bowels of the earth. The going up and down is most dangerous, for they come up with their sack of metal tied to their backs, which takes four or five hours, step by step, and if they make the slightest false step they may fall 700 feet. And when they arrive at the top, weary and out of breath, they find a mine owner who scolds them because they did not come up quickly enough, or because they did not bring enough load, and for the slightest reason makes them go back down again."

In their zeal to gain greater wealth even more quickly, many Spanish mine owners purchased Negro slaves from Africa, but they were expensive, costing several hundred dollars each, and they did not adapt well to the mines, so most African slaves were worked on plantations or rancherias in the mountains, while the Indian, whose numbers seemed inexhaustible, were forced to labor in the deep shafts and tunnels. Pereira compared the plight of the Indian with that of the Negro. "The African slaves may esteem themselves lucky by comparison, and their lot is envied by the Indians, who the king so often has said should be free. This state of affairs is due to the insatiable hunger for wealth of those who govern the Indians."

Closely guarded by his Spanish overlord, who was armed with firearms which could kill him instantly, the Indian had no choice but to labor his life away. And if he failed to do so, severe punishment was swift and certain, as was further described. "The custom to condemn Indians to those abominable places is to send them to their death. One often meets on the roads, Indians tied by their hair to the tail of a horse, by which a mestizo (a trusted half-breed) drags them to the works. The Indian has only one master, the mine owner, who most scandalous of all is often a priest or minister of worship. All of them, including the priests, treat the defenseless Indian more inhumanely than the worst that can be imagined against Negro slaves. Punishment for their crimes are usually for being rebellious, and their punishment is often by burning them, by nailing them down on the ground with forked sticks on every limb, and then applying the fire by degrees, from the feet and hands, burning them gradually up to the head, whereby their pains are extravagant."

The Dominican Priest Bartolome de Los Casas wrote: "They erected a gallows low enough so that the poor tormented creatures might touch the ground with their feet, and strung up thirteen Indians, affirming that they did it in honor of Our

Redeemer. Then putting fire under them, they burned the poor wretchs alive. Those they took pity on and were able to spare, they sent away with their hands cut off." It is little wonder the Indians had no interest in learning Christianity from the Spaniards.

Few priests and even fewer mine owners dared speak out in defense of the Indian. One who did was the already mentioned Father Los Casas, who in a letter written to Bishop Cabedo in 1519 said: "I am one of the oldest immigrants of the Indies, where I have spent many years, and where I saw and came into contact with the cruelties which have been inflicted on those peaceful and gentle people, cruelties more atrocious and unnatural than any recorded of untutored and savage barbarians. No other reason can be assigned for them than the greed for gold by our countrymen. In wicked and unjust wars, numberless Indians, living at peace in their own homes, without molesting anyone, were slaughtered. And what kind of arms did the Indians have? Their arms were about as useless as bulrushes. And when the Spaniards saw this, they came with their horsemen, well armed with swords and lances, making a cruel havoc and slaughter among them, sparing neither sex nor age. Their country, which formerly teemed with people and cities has been made desolate. Further, by enslaving the common people after doing away with their chiefs and leaders, they are divided out in Encomiendas of 50 and 100 and cast into the mines, where overwhelmed by incredible labor, they perished. They died wherever they come into contact with the Spanish."

Action on his pleas was slow in coming, but Bishop Cabedo relayed his letter to the Pope, and on June 17th, 1537, the Bull Sublimis Deus Sic Dilexit from Pope Paul III himself directed that the Indians were the children of God, and were not to be enslaved. The Pope declared that the Indians were men, and were not sub-human. They were not to be called dogs, nor beat with sticks or whips. By Royal Decree, on November 20th, 1542, the New Laws of the Indies were ordered by King Charles I, directing the good treatment and care of the Indians. But protests from rich mine owners, many of them priests, that mining would cease and with it the King's one-fifth share of gold and silver, quickly changed minds at the Royal Court. Three years later the Encomienda system allowing Indian slaves was reinstated, never to be stopped again until the end of the Mexican revolution, nearly 300 years later.

Meanwhile Francisco Pizarro waged war on the Inca nation, where he found even greater wealth than Cortez had in Mexico. The similarities of their expeditions are amazing. With only 170 soldiers and 60 horses (Cortez had 400 men with 16 horses) Pizarro attacked the army of Emperor Atahualpa, and by the use of his armor, firearms and horses defeated Indian warriors numbered in the thousands. And just as Cortez had done, Pizarro held the Inca Emperor for ransom. Atahualpa ordered that his cell, a room 15' by 25' in size, be filled with gold, and that two other rooms of equal size be filled with silver. His treasure was even greater than Montezuma's, and Pizarro soon collected a huge amount of gold, in the form of statues, ornaments and plates from temple walls, as well as a huge gold chain 700 feet long, weighing ten tons!

In his True Account of New Castile, Pizarro wrote: "We saw a well built house entirely plated with gold, measuring 350 paces from corner to corner. From it we took down 700 gold plates, while from another we pulled plates weighing 200,000 pesos. A Chief came in bringing another 700 plates of gold and much silver, an account of which was taken, and it was found to total 326,000 pesos of pure gold. The King's share of all the treasure amounted to 262,000 pesos of pure gold, while of silver, 10,000 marcs formed the Royal Fifth."

Pizarro added: "In one day we melted 80,000 pesos of gold, which was done by the Indians who have many good smelters and silversmiths. I cannot recount all the different shapes and pieces of gold we melted. There was a throne of gold which weighed eight arrobas (200 pounds), worth 25,000 pesos. There were two sacks of gold, each equal to two fanegas (bushels) of wheat, and an idol the size of a child four years of age." Note that just as Cortez had his loot melted into bars at an Indian smelter, so too did Pizarro have his treasure smelted by Indian silversmiths.

Four galleons heavily laden with silver and gold sailed to Seville, and counting only the value of gold which had been cast into bars, "but not

vases, ornaments and personal gold," the king's share equalled "708,580 pesos, each peso being valued at 450 maravedis, or all equal to 318,860,000 maravedis. The silver was 49,000 marcs, each equal to eight ounces, or 108,307,000 maravedis of silver."

At Cajamarca, Pizarro had the Emperor Atahualpa strangled and hid his body. With 7,000 Indians, each carrying 75 pounds of treasure, including the golden chain 700 feet long, he began the long journey to Cuzco, the capital. But when the Indians learned that their Emperor had been murdered, they revolted and attacked the Spaniards. Pizarro and his soldiers were forced to flee, driving as many Indian treasure bearers as possible ahead of them. Most of the vast Inca treasure was lost, some of it thrown into Lake Guatavita, but still Pizarro was able to save and later send a fabulous fortune of gold and silver to Spain.

In 1545 an attempt to drain Lake Guatavita was made by a bucket brigade using Indian labor. The shoreline was actually dropped ten feet in three months, and many of the priceless golden artifacts were recovered. After the days of Spanish colonialism was ended, treasure salvors recovered even more of the golden hoard, and today literally tons of gleaming golden breast plates, stunning masks and glittering bracelets, head-dresses, idols and countless other skillfully crafted archaeological wonders are on display at the national museum at Bogota, Columbia.

Strangely, one of Pizarro's soldiers, Juan Valverde, later returned and married an Indian woman, and in time he was accepted by the Indians and was shown where some of the royal treasure was hidden. When the opportunity came, Valverde took some of the treasure and returned to Spain, where he lived in great luxury. He freely described where the treasure was hidden, but having no need for greater wealth, never returned to New Spain. The great cache has never been found since, and is remembered today as Valverde's Treasure. Perhaps somewhere in the Spanish archives, Valverde's waybill to the lost treasure cache might still be found.

Although Balboa, Cortez and Pizarro had discovered unknown kingdoms and wealth which staggered the imagination, they had not found

Cibola, according to legend the richest of all lands. In 1530 Governor Nuno de Guzman learned from an Indian slave that Cibola was far to the north of Mexico, in a land where there was a great lake with Indian cities built around it. Tejo told the Governor, "When I was a little boy my father was a trader, and he travelled over the interior selling feathers which were used for head-dresses. He traded them for gold, which was very plentiful in that region. I went with my father once or twice and I saw towns as large as Mexico City. There were seven of them, and in them there were rows of streets inhabited by workers in gold and silver. To reach these towns we crossed a great desert for forty days, where there was no vegetation for our livestock except some very short grass." During the next several years Governor Guzman personally led or dispatched exploring expeditions north from Mexico City, and although he did not find Cibola anywhere in the deserts of Sonora or what would become Arizona and New Mexico, his men did map the country for 600 miles beyond what was then known. They also established outposts and mission-visitas as far north as Culiacan. Their blazed paths was the start of the Old Spanish Trail. Then came an event which would quickly open the entire north country to exploration and settlement.

In June, 1527, the Panfilo de Narvaez expedition of four ships and 400 men was shipwrecked on the coast of Florida. After continual battles with the Indians, only four men remained alive, and they survived only by fleeing into the swamps, saving nothing but the clothes on their backs. They included the expedition's secretary, Cabeza de Vaca, Castillo de Maldonado, Dorantes de Carranza and a Negro slave named Esteban, who was owned by Dorantes. For eight years they wandered through the unknown wilderness under the harshest of conditions. They journeyed along the gulf coast to Texas, turned northward through New Mexico and Arizona, perhaps as far north as the Grand Canyon, and then wandered south to the Sea of Cortez, separating Mexico from Baja, California. The details of their arduous journey need not concern us here, but the amazing tale they told when they staggered into the northern outpost of Culiacan in May, 1536, certainly does.

The four survivors of the Narvaez expedition had survived the most awful hardships, often serving as slaves to various Indian bands or being sold or traded from tribe to tribe. Only the fact that they were able to act as medicine men to the Indians, setting broken bones or treating injuries and sickness kept them from being killed. Also, the Indians were in awe of Esteban, the giant Negro, for they had never seen a black man. For most of the time they lived on scraps thrown away or on pieces of raw meat they took from wild beasts. But of greater interest to Governor Guzman than their tales of hardship was a small copper bell carried by Dorantes and the stories of treasure told by De Vaca.

During their exodus in the wilderness, an Indian had given Dorantes a small copper bell which had a human face etched on it. Dorantes said that the Indian had told him the bell had come "from the far north where there was much of the same metal." Those who examined the bell concluded that wherever it had comed from, "there must be foundries, for the metal had been cast in a mold." To excite Governor Guzman even further, De Vaca reported that often the Indians had told him of a rich land of great cities to the north, "where people lived in populous towns with very large houses, where copper, gold and silver were plentiful, and where they traded turquoise and emeralds for the plumage of parrots." It was the same story that the slave Tejo had already told the Governor, so he lost no time readying another expedition to investigate the strange tale he had been told. Surely, Cibola must be somewhere very close by.

CHAPTER FOUR

IN SEARCH OF CIBOLA

"I tell you, gold is more plentiful there, then copper is with us!"

—Tales Of A Conquistadore

From the time of Columbus, the Spaniard's first interest was always gold. Father Perez de Ribas, Padre Provincial of all New Spain made that quite clear in his writings. "The first motive for the entry of Spaniards into the sierras was to search for silver, many rich deposits soon being found. The sierras extend north from the city of Guadalajara for 300 leagues and more, far into New Mexico, but they would never have been explored had not there existed the ever tantalizing hope of discovering vast riches, the hope which draws men irresistably, even from across the reaches of the unknown seas. The discovery of those riches is most satisfying to the king."

Among the first to follow De Vaca's trail north were Juan de Asuncion and Fray Pedro Nadal. Poorly equipped, they never ventured far, nevertheless, they pushed the trail a little further into the unknown and returned with tales that the Indians they met wore cotton clothing and owned great quantities of turquoise. In November, 1538, Viceroy Mendoza himself directed Father Marcos de Niza, an Italian Franciscan, to investigate De Vaca's story. The Viceroy instructed Father Marcos to take samples of precious metals and gemstones to compare with those the Indians might have, telling him to "bring back samples of everything precious, so that His Majesty might be fully informed." How Father Marcos ever became ordained as a man of God remains somewhat of a mystery, for he proved to be one of the greatest liars of all time!

Father Marcos began his journey to Cibola on March 7th, 1539, with the giant Negro Esteban as his guide. The story of how Esteban was killed by Indians at a Zuni pueblo and how Father Marcos saw the pueblo only from a distance need not be repeated at length, only the report he brought back to Viceroy Mendoza concerns us now. Father Marcos returned to Culiacan on September 2nd, 1539, and gave a report entirely fabricated from his fertile imagination. "When I showed the natives the samples of gold I had taken with me, they said there were vessels of it among their people, and that they wore round ornaments of it hanging from their noses and ears, and also that they have blades of gold with which they scrape the sweat from their bodies. Many of the people I saw there wore silk clothing down to their feet. Of the richness of that country I cannot write, because it is so great it does not seem possible. They have temples of metal covered with precious stones, I think emeralds. They use vessels of gold and silver because they have no other metal!"

So great was the excitement caused by the report of Father Marcos that Culiacan was deserted almost overnight. Expeditions not authorized by Viceroy Mendoza were illegal, nevertheless, almost every able-bodied man joined the rush to the new El Dorado. Melchior Diaz with a party of 15 men was one of the first to leave. It is now known that Diaz travelled north as far as the Tizon (Colorado) River, to a place not described precisely, but thought to be along that section now known as the Grand Canyon. But the Diaz party, and many others whose identities were never known or recorded, have been over-shadowed by the greatest journey of exploration the west ever witnessed, that of Francisco Coronado. There was never a conquest like that of Coronado in the history of the world. In less than a decade he conquered more new territory for Spain than the Roman Empire acquired in five centuries! Since Coronado's saga opened the American West and gave birth to countless tales of treasure and lost mines, it is pertinent to describe it in some detail.

On January 6th, 1540, Francisco Vasquez de Coronado, Governor of Nueva Galicia, was commissioned by King Charles I as Captain-General of the Indies, with specific instructions to find and explore the Land of Cibola. Garcia Lopez de Cardenas was chosen as his Maestro de Campo, or second in command, while Don Pedro de Tovar was designated as Ensign General. Pedro Castenada was picked to be chronicler of the expedition. Father Marcos reluctantly accompanied the party, but only because he was ordered to do so. He knew there were no golden cities to be found, and he dreaded what might happen when only a few poor Zuni pueblos were discovered. He had good reason to worry.

Translations of Castenada's journal differ slightly, but it is generally agreed that Coronado's army consisted of some 250 mounted men and 62 foot soldiers. Most were outfitted with the best available castillian armor and swords. Included in the armament were 19 crossbows and 27 harquebus firearms. Several hundred Indian slaves accompanied the army as servants and herdsmen for the approximately 1,000 cattle, sheep and hogs driven along for food. The great expedition left the outpost town of Compostela on February 23rd, 1540, following the already well travelled Spanish Trail northward. It had been used by Cabeza de Vaca, Father Marcos, Melchior Diaz and a host of other unknown frontiersmen who had joined the rush to Cibola, or to prospect for mines and hunt for slaves. Coronado would find Diaz along the Gila River in Arizona, and Diaz would accompany him on his quest to the north.

Coronado's army slowly made its way north into Arizona, where it followed the Gila River to the northeast. The trail was easy to follow into the land of the Zuni Indians, where Esteban had been killed and Father Marcos had seen the mud pueblos which he told Viceroy Mendoza were splendid cities. Instead of Cibola, Coronado found only a

The New Spain of Coronado's time. Utah Lake (Copalla) draining into the Pacific, and California still shown as an island.

squalid huddle of stone and adobe tenement like houses, "looking as if they had been all crumpled up together." At Hawikuh Pueblo they were met by the same angry Indians who had killed Esteban. They threw heavy stones down on the Spaniards and fired flights of arrows at them. Coronado was struck by a heavy stone and was knocked senseless. His soldiers attacked and seized the pueblo, killing many Indians.

They found nothing at Hawikuh or any of the surrounding pueblos which even remotely resembled anything described by Father Marcos. Because of the great anger of the soldiers, Castenada wrote: "When we first saw the villages that Father Marcos said was Cibola, such were the curses that were hurled at him that I pray God may protect him from them!" Because Coronado feared for the priest's life, he sent him back to Mexico with a report to the viceroy, in which he wrote, "We are very distrustful of him and feel great anxiety and dismay to see that everything is just the opposite of what he has told Your Lordship." At Culiacan, Father Marcos fell into disgrace with the viceroy and was reassigned to a desert visita at Jolap, where he died in poverty in 1558.

Coronado's soldiers searched every pueblo at Cibola for treasure, but none was to be found. In the expedition's journal Castenada wrote: "Of gems, only two fragments of emerald and some little brown stones which approach the color of poor garnet have been found. There is little turquoise, for most of it has been hidden. As for gold and silver, some very small pieces have been found, which those who know about minerals say is not bad. I have not been able to learn where they obtained it, for they refuse to tell the truth in anything." Apparently the soldiers tried every means to make the Indians tell where the tiny flakes of gold came from, and we can well imagine the methods they used, for Castenada continued, "We have not yet managed to induce the Indians to tell, but I trust in God they will not be able to avoid answering much longer!" The Indians insisted they had no gold, and anxious to be rid of the Spaniards, they told of rich lands further north where gold was plentiful, to the west at Tusayan, and to the northeast at Quivera. Coronado quickly dispatched exploring parties to find those new lands.

In his History of Utah, Hubert H. Bancroft wrote: "As Coronado was journeying to the north, he rested at Cibola, that is to say at Zuni, and while waiting for the main part of his army, he sent expeditions out in several directions. Pedro de Tovar with twenty men and attended by Fray Juan de Padilla, proceeded north-westward, and after five days reached Tusayan, or the Moqui villages, which were quickly captured. There they learned of a large river further north." While at Tusayan sometime in July, 1540, the soldiers encountered a band of friendly Zunis, from whom they learned of a rich province far to the northwest, across deserts and mountains, where the people lived on the shore of a great lake and owned much gold and silver. Always there was the story that the mines were still further north, but now Coronado learned of another land even richer than Cibola, a land which would tantalize treasure hunters for the next century. It was the fabled land of Teguayo, far to the north by the shores of a great lake the Indians called Copalla.

Pedro de Tovar and his men returned to Hawikuh on August 25th, 1540, reporting that he had reached Tusayan, a scenic land, but he brought back no gold. He also related that the Indians there had told him of a land of treasure far to the north, at a place they called Teguayo. Immediately Coronado dispatched Captain Cardenas with 25 men to locate that promised land. Pedro de Sotomayor went along as the expeditions chronicler. Cardenas was ordered to explore further north than De Tovar had, Coronado allowing him "80 days to go and return, to search for gold, not scenery!" Historian Bancroft states that the Cardenas party were the first Europeans to enter what is now Utah.

"With an ample supply of provisions, Cardenas marched for 20 days through a desert country until he discovered a river. It was a branch of the river called Tizon (Colorado) and it flowed to the southwest. In vain for days they sought to escape from the mountains and descend to the river, for they were suffering greatly from thirst. At length three of the lightest and most active crept over the bank and descended into the canyon until they were out of sight. They did not return until evening when they reported their failure to reach the river, saying that everything was much further

away than it seemed from above. Rocks which looked no larger than a man were in fact higher than the great cathedral at Seville." Compelled by thirst, they were forced to return to Cibola, the Hawikuh publo.

Bancroft cites records in the Archives of The Indies at Seville which reveal that Cardenas travelled north to the San Juan River in southeastern Utah, and followed it downstream to the Tizon or Colorado. If Cardenas had travelled west beyond Tusayan, Zuni, as some suppose, he would have crossed the Little Colorado River, which his chronicler, Sotomayor, does not mention. In fact, Sotomayor recorded they suffered greatly from thirst, something he would not have written had they reached the Little Colorado. Bancroft states that Cardenas viewed the Colorado at a place much nearer to its source than had Diaz, although the Indians encountered belonged to the same nation as those Diaz had met. In The Founding of Utah, author Levi Edgar Young concurs with Bancroft, also stating that Cardenas was the first European of record to enter present day Utah. Of interest is the fact that several pieces of armor of the type used by Cardenas, but not used after 1600 were found in the Monument Valley area in 1952.

Some believe that several of the Cardenas party explored even further north, crossing the San Juan and wintering somewhere in the land of Teguayo. In his journals compiled from 1595 to 1645, a time when the facts are much clearer than they are now, Jesuit Padre Perez de Ribas wrote: "They finally arrived at forty degrees north latitude, where in winter it was so cold that the rivers were frozen over. They crossed a country where the Indians passed their days hunting the cibolos (buffalos)." It is interesting to note that forty degrees north latitude passes through what is now Utah Valley and Utah Lake, known in the sixteenth century as Lake Copalla and the Land of Teguayo!

On his return to Hawikuh, Cardenas found the Indians on the verge of revolt because of the abuses they had suffered and the large quantities of corn and other foodstuffs which had been stolen from them. Two hundred of the Indians were captured, and because Coronado had ordered that they were not to be taken alive, but an example of them should be made so that the other Indians would fear the Spaniards, Cardenas ordered that 200 stakes be prepared to burn them alive. When the Indians saw what was planned they ran to escape. "Our men attacked on all sides, so that there was great confusion, and the horsemen gave chase to those who tried to escape. As the country was level, not a man of them remained alive." But several other Indians did flee during the night, so that news of the Spaniard's cruelty soon spread throughout the land. When the Indians of other villages learned of Coronado's obsession with gold and of his cruel treatment of their countrymen, they saw a means of getting rid of him. So that the Spaniards would not stop at their pueblos, Indians would tell Coronado that Cibola lay still further ahead, always somewhere else.

Because Cardenas had been unable to cross the Tizon River in his quest for Teguayo, when spring came Coronado led his army to the northeast in search of Quivera. The Indians of Zuni were eager to tell him whatever he wanted to hear of the riches to be found there, so that they might be rid of him. Coronado was told that in Quivera there were great quantities of turquoise, and that objects of silver were commonplace. He was told that the people of Quivera lived by the side of a great river, where fishes were as big as horses, and where the people used large canoes which carried great sails. "Gold is so plentiful that the natives, not knowing of any other metal, make everything they need from it, even the tips of their arrows and lances. The Chief of that land wears a copper plate over his breast and takes his afternoon nap under a great tree on which are hung many little golden bells, which lull him to sleep as they swing in the breeze." And to Coronado their tales seemed to be true, for hadn't Cabeza de Vaca returned with just such a bell?

During April, 1541, Coronado started for Quivera, "A land with gold, silver and fabrics, abundant and beautiful in everything!" He passed by the Manzano and Sandia mountains where he saw "old mines of turquoise," but they appeared to be ancient and long unworked even then. At one village along the way his soldiers "found ollas filled with a shiny metal used by the Indians in glazing their pottery, which is an indication that mines of silver can be found in that country." The "shiny metal" was probably mica or galena lead, pretty,

but of little value.

All summer long the ragged army pushed further northeast in search of Quivera, lured on by tales told by Indians anxious to have them pass through their country as quickly as possible. They crossed all of New Mexico, passed through northern Texas into Oklahoma, and continued far out onto the barren plains of Kansas. Castenada recorded, "All there is at Quivera is a very brutish people, without any decency whatever, in their homes or in anything." It was fortunate that Father Marcos had returned to Mexico, for soldiers cursed him daily. With another bleak winter facing him and supplies running low, Coronado began the long journey back to Culiacan. To his king he wrote: "As far as I can judge, it does not appear to me that there is any hope of finding gold or silver, but I trust in God that if there is any, we shall get our share of it, and it shall not escape us through any lack of diligence in the search."

At Cibola (Zuni) three Franciscan Priests asked permission to remain and establish a mission to instruct the Indians in the ways of Christianity. They were Fray Juan de Padilla, Fray Luis de Escalona and Fray Juan de la Cruz. Coronado's army was hardly out of sight before all three were killed by the Indians. Three Indian guides also remained behind, Andres of Culiacan, Gaspar of Mexico City and Anton of Guadalajara. They were more fortunate, for when the Espejo expedition passed through Zuni more than forty years later, all three were still alive and had families.

Coronado was not as lucky as his guides, for on his return to Mexico he was arrested. He had opened a land as vast as any conquistadore ever had, but he had found no gold. Too much money and too many lives had been spent for nothing. Although in time the charges against him were dismissed, he died in disgrace and was buried in the walls of the Church of Santo Domingo at Mexico City. Cardenas fared no better, for he had brought back no gold either. He was arrested, banned from the new world and sentenced to exile in Spain. But the Coronado expedition had opened a whole new world where others would find treasure. Castenada described the real value of their great odyssey when he wrote, "Although they found not the gold for which they sought, better still, they found a place in which to search!"

CHAPTER FIVE

THE MINER'S BIBLE

"Gold! Gold! Gold! Gold!
Bright and yellow, hard and cold.
Molten, graven, hammered, rolled,
Heavy to get and light to hold!"

—Thomas Hood

While Coronado's army was marching across Arizona and New Mexico and exploring eastward into Oklahoma and Kansas, others were also seeking the riches of Teguayo. Hernando de Alarcon sailed north through the Sea of Cortez to the mouth of the Colorado River, which he was able to navigate to present day Yuma and the Gila River. From there his men explored into the land of the Ammachabas, the Mojaves, in hope of joining forces with Coronado. Alarcon's ship carried supplies for his army, it then being believed that the Colorado and Cibola were only a few days journey apart, but unknown to Alarcon, Coronado was by then far to the northeast. During his voyage Alarcon left behind a small treasure of historical significance. His ship, the Santa Catalina, became "unduly frightened" in a sudden storm, and Alarcon had thrown overboard "nine cannons, two anchors and many other indispensable things." They have never been found, and if recovered would be of great value to a museum.

While Coronado and Alarcon were seeking Cibola, the story of Hernando DeSoto's forced march from Florida to the Mississippi River became known in The Discovery and Conquest of Tiarra, in which it was reported that both mines of gold and golden cities existed in the north, in the Land of Polinecia. After having been Pizarro's chief lieutenant in the conquest of Peru, DeSoto went on to other adventures. In May, 1539, with a fleet of ten ships, 600 men and 200 horses he landed on the coast of Florida, not far from where Cabeza de Vaca began his long walk to Culiacan in 1527. With his army, DeSoto marched to the Rio Meschacebe, which he crossed and explored into Arkansas and Oklahoma. Failing to find any cities of gold, he engaged in a dreadful war against the Indians and was forced back to the Mississippi, where his army became lost in the swamps. There,

with no hope of rescue, DeSoto "sank into a deep despondency" and died of fever, probably malaria, and was buried in the river to keep his body from falling into the hands of the Indians. His golden cities of "Polinecia" were never found, but their reported existence added to the hope of finding mines of gold somewhere in the north.

During the same period two even more important books were hand-written by Fray Bernardino de Sahagun, *The Dictionary of Earthly Things* and the *Historia de Mexico*. Eight copies of each were copied by hand, but all except one of each was lost when a ship on which they were being carried sank while en route to Spain. The only remaining copies were "lost" in mission archives for 200 years. Sahagun's books told of Indian mines and mining before the Spanish conquest, particularly the turquoise mines of New Mexico, some the very same ones seen by Coronado.

Almost every new expedition journeying into the north encountered Indians who told them of rich mines and wealthy nations further north, always near Lake Copalla in the land called Teguayo, said to be the ancient home of the Aztecs. One of the early searchers was Francisco de Ibarra, who in 1565 led a campaign north in search of Teguayo, "into the land of the Yutahs." It is difficult to retrace his route from what little is known of his march, but in those days the "Yutahs" were located in southern Colorado and in Utah north of the San Juan River. By the mid-sixteenth century British fur trappers had explored across Canada and southward into the northern Rockies and into the land of the Utes. Their interests were in peltries, not gold, but they reported meeting the Spanish even at that early date and noted their preoccupation with the precious metals. In his *Principal Navigations, Voyages and Discoveries of the English Nation,* published in 1572, Richard Akluyt wrote: "The Spaniards have notice of seven cities which old men among the Indians tell them are in the far north. They use daily much diligence in seeking them, but they cannot find any of them. They say that the witchcraft of the Indians is such that when they come near these towns, a mist is cast upon them so that they cannot be seen." Before the end of the sixteenth century, French explorers also noted the presence of Spanish miners in the northern mountains, and more than a few of the Frenchmen caught the mining fever from the Spaniards and became treasure hunters themselves.

That vast quantities of gold and silver were shipped to Spain from the northernmost border-lands of New Mexico, then all of the lands north of the Rio Grande and west of the Rockies, cannot be doubted. Even though records of the wealth shipped from individual mines were not kept, or if they were have since become lost, the totals received at Seville are on record, and they are staggering. And those totals represent only the small part that was the King's Quinto, or treasure declared as personal wealth, but did not include that which was smuggled in illegally. From the time of Columbus in 1492 to that of Cortez in 1521, some $20,000,000 was sent to Spain, with at least $10,000,000 being shipped every year thereafter. During the first century of Spanish exploitation, Baron Von Humboldt placed the value of gold and silver shipped to Spain at $1,000,000,000, while a Spanish historian stated it represented "$448,000,000 pesos del oro."

Plate fleets, flotillas of galleons heavily laden with treasure, sailed for Spain nearly every year, but many of the ships were seized by French or English pirates, while almost countless others were sunk in Caribbean hurricanes. They sailed from ports as far south as Tampico and Veracruz, as well as from now unused harbors along the gulf coast near present Galveston and Padre Island. Of 76 galleons bound for Spain in 1520, only 37 arrived at Seville, in 1545 only 38 of 97, in 1550 only 81 of 135 and in 1555 only 44 of 65. Pirates claimed almost as much Spanish gold as was lost in hurricanes, but so lucrative were the mines in the lands of the "Yutahs" that the risks involved were still worthwhile, at least to the king.

In 1592 the Spanish treasure ship Madre de Dios, carrying $4,000,000 in declared gold and probably as much more in undisclosed cargo was captured by an English man of war. A Dutch pirate, who Admiral Don Juan Torres called Pie de Palo because of his wooden leg, ran the admiral's ship aground and seized all of his treasure, "even to a chest containing gold chains, diamonds, pearls and precious stones," which a returning priest had hidden to avoid paying the Royal Fifth. When the priest arrived at Seville, "He was imprisoned, went mad and was beheaded."

As early as 1511 Spanish mining laws had been formulated for the new world. Mining had provided a large part of the Spanish economy for centuries. Spanish miners had long been employed as supervisors and engineers at the rich mines of Saxony and Briton, and even before that at those of the Roman Empire. Their methods were primitive by modern standards, employing the use of dowsing, pendulums and dip needles, yet it can't be denied that the richest ore veins ever found in New Spain and New Mexico were located by those methods. Using no other instruments, Spanish miners uncovered rich ore bodies from Mexico to the northern Rockies. By their own records, incomplete and often falsified to avoid paying the Royal Fifth, from 1492 to 1820, when the last Plate Fleet sailed, they shipped more than ten billion dollars worth of bullion to Spain, more gold than was possessed by all other nations combined, and two-thirds of the world's silver! A closer look at those primitive methods is in order.

Dowsing, the art of using directional locators, is the oldest known method of searching for mineral veins or buried treasure. The Spanish miners used dowsing extensively in their search for precious metals. Dowsing is based on the principle of radiesthesia, the science of detecting radiation given off by all minerals, even though they are beyond the limitations of normal perception. Each mineral emits radiation of a particular wavelength, which is intercepted by the operator through his dowsing rod. Dowsing rods may be elaborate and contain a sample of the mineral being sought, but most Spanish miners used only a forked limb or small branch of a supple tree, such as a willow or birch. The forked limb would bend or point in the direction of the ore vein, and would dip when the user passed directly over the vein or ore body.

Dowsing is a very old science. In an Arabic manuscript dated before the time of Mohammed, it is written: "When the Queen of Sheba came to visit King Solomon, she had among her train diviners who dowsed for gold." In another ancient manuscript there is a story of a city without water, where dowsers of that day located water by dowsing over maps. Marco Polo observed the use of dowsing rods in China during the thirteenth century. An early English book states: "The practice of dowsing in England has been used for a very long time. One of the first references to dowsing was recorded in the fifteenth century when German dowsers were employed to locate some lost tin mines in Cornwall, at which time the inhabitants learned the art from them." That may be the earliest reference ever made to a lost mine. In 1622, King Charles II organized the Royal Society of London, and one of its first published works discussed the use of dowsing to locate minerals. In the museum of science at Kensington, England, there is a collection of dowing rods which were used in England in 1664. An even earlier vignette etched on ivory depicts a man using a dowsing rod and another using a pendulum.

The Spanish were very skilled in the use of the pendulum, a metal needle or weight suspended by a thread, which would swing back and forth to guide the user to a mineral vein, and rotate in a circular motion when directly over the vein. The so-called dip needles often referred to in Spanish mining records were in fact four small forked rods, usually four to six inches in length, having a forked end. They were especially advantageous for seeking buried treasure as opposed to finding mineral veins, but their great disadvantage was that they required two persons to operate them, each person holding a needle in each hand. They required considerable skill to use, in order for two operators to move in coordination over rough ground, keeping all four needles in contact with each other. When successfully manipulated, the needles will move either left or right, or up and down to indicate the direction of the treasure being sought. Neither the pendulum or the dip needle were used as extensively as the dowsing rod, but we cannot doubt the effectiveness of any of those instruments, for by their use Spanish miners discovered nearly every major ore body or vein in the regions where they explored.

Until 1555 there was no written textbook for miners and prospectors, but in that year there appeared a book which was to become the miner's bible for the next 250 years. Its title was *De Re Metaliica*, and it was written by George Bauer, whose name was usually spelled in Latin as Georgius Agricola. It described every facet of mining, from prospecting for ore veins, smelting and milling to the authority of the mine owner. "To the mining prefect whom the King appoints, all men of all races, age and rank must give submission and obedience. He governs and regulates everything at his discretion, lays down the law and gives orders as a magistrate, levies penalties and punishs offenders, and throws into prison men who are fraudulent, dissolute or negligent." Agricola even described the use of slaves in the mines, something the Spanish already knew well.

De Re Metallica described the use of slaves in great detail. "There is a place full of rich gold mines, out of which with the pains of many laborers gold is dug. For the King condemns to those mines notorious criminals, captives taken in war and persons often falsely accused, and not only themselves but sometimes all of their family are sent to work there, to punish them and to advance the profit of the King. Bound in fetters, they are thrust into the mines where they work continually without rest, either day or night. They set over them barbarians who at the very nod of the mine owner lashes them severely. No care at all is taken of the bodies of these poor creatures, so that they have not a rag to cover their nakedness. For though they are sick, maimed or lame, no rest in the least is allowed them, neither the weakness of old age nor womens infirmities excuse them, but all are driven to their work with blows and cudgelling, until at length, overborne with the intolerable weight of their misery, they drop down dead, so that these miserable creatures always expect the future to be more terrible than even the present, and therefore long for death as more desireable than life." With *De Re Metallica* as their guide, the Indians of the Americas suffered terrible abuses at the hands of the Spanish.

Many of the mining methods described by Agricola have never been improved on greatly since his work appeared, except that now most of his machines are driven by engine power, not manpower. Agricola's text was probably the most important book in New Spain, perhaps even more widely read than the Holy Bible. His book was heavily illustrated, and although he did not recommend using "the enchanted twig" for dowsing, nevertheless, its use is demonstrated in many of his illustrations. Agricola described the use of dowsing rods for each type of metal being sought, stating miners use the forked limb of a hazel tree to locate silver, forked twigs of ash for copper and pitch pine for lead, but notes that they use rods of iron to locate gold.

Before the publication of *De Re Metallica,* ore was crushed by a large boulder which was lashed to the end of a long pole, which was supported near its center by an upright post. The boulder was raised by leverage of the pole and then allowed to drop onto the ore, which had been placed in a hollowed out stone mortar. It was powered by the hardest kind of hand labor. After *De Re Metallica* appeared, the arrastra became the principle method of crushing ore for the next several hundred years. The arrastra could be built almost anywhere of materials already at hand, and was reasonably effective at crushing ore. In many parts of the west it was used until well into the twentieth century. The arrastra consisted of a circular shallow pit or vat with flat stones closely fitted together along its bottom. A heavy stone was dragged around the vat, at the end of a chain or rope tied to a cross beam which was supported at its center by an upright post. One or two men, usually slaves, grasped the opposite end of the cross beam and walked around the vat, pulling the heavy drag-stone behind them. A horse could also be used, but at the Spanish mines, men were cheaper than horses.

The ore was first broken into small pieces by slaves using stone hammers, and was then dropped into the vat where it was crushed to the size of grains of sand by the drag-stone. If available, a small flow of water was fed into the vat, which carried the lighter sand out through a discharge hole, leaving the heavier metal particles behind. Each arrastra could crush about a ton of ore every day. If quicksilver was available, it was sprinkled into the vat to absorb the gold, forming an amalgam. The amalgam was then roasted in a pan

in which salt had been added, over an open fire, which evaporated the quicksilver and left the pure gold. The process, called amalgamation, was perfected by Ferdanez de Velasco. Approximately one pound of quicksilver was lost for every pound of gold recovered. The Indians forced to walk in the vat and pull the heavy drag-stone were soon poisoned by quicksilver entering their bodies through the skin of their feet, as were those who breathed the fumes of the quicksilver being evaporated from the roasted ore.

In *De Re Metallica*, Agricola left no doubt that mining was a dangerous occupation, even in the most carefully operated mines. "Miners are sometimes killed by the pestilential air, sometimes their lungs rot away, sometimes they perish by being crushed in masses of fallen rock, sometimes falling from ladders into the shaft they break their arms, legs or necks. The dust of the mines has corrosive qualities, it eats away the lungs and implants consumption in the body. At the mines there are women who have married seven husbands, all of whom have been carried off to a premature death. For if a man mines, he may be alive one hour and dead the next." The life expectancy of Indian slave laborers was only a few months, but there were lots of Indians, at least for awhile.

The appearance of *De Re Metallica* and the renewed interest in mining it caused resulted in the discovery of a new milling process at the Spanish mines. Called the patio process, it allowed miners to sink their shafts much deeper into the earth. Before its invention, silver could only be recovered if it was dug from oxidized ore in shallow surface workings, but the patio process allowed the miner to mine silver from the richer sulphide ores found at greater depth. The ore was ground into a fine sand in an arrastra and then spread over a flat stone patio where salt, quicksilver and copper sulfate (obtained by roasting copper-iron ore) was poured over it. Indian laborers were used to mix the whole together, with their hands and by trampling it with their feet. They kept turning it in the hot sun for approximately two months until it turned to a gray color, after which it was washed and the quicksilver roasted off over an open fire, leaving the silver behind.

The loss of quicksilver, much of which was

brought from Spain, was high, but the death rate of the Indians was even higher. The problem became so acute that in 1556, King Phillip II ordered that "Strenuous efforts should be made to find mines of quicksilver, owing to the great need for it in New Granada, and the high price it brings."

CHAPTER SIX

THE OLD TRAIL NORTH

"What have these mountains worth revealing?
More glory and more grief than I can tell!"

—Emily Bronte

After Francisco de Ibarra's journey of 1565 "into the land of the Yutahs," many other expeditions travelled north, most of them illegal and unrecorded. Only the trails they left and the places where they cut their names and dates and a few rusting artifacts remain to show they passed that way. In 1580 Francisco Sanchez Chamuscado accompanied by Fray Augustin Rodriguez made a year long trek into the unknown. On their way north they carved their names into the soft sandstone of Morro Rock, 38 miles west of present Grants, New Mexico, where they can still be seen today. Fray Rodriguez noted the furs which Indians were wearing, but recorded that they were more interested in other wealth. "There was more spectacular wealth than furs, and our energies were bent to exploring for gold and silver." Captain Chamuscada wrote, "In the Sierra Ladrone and San Mateo Mountains we found many very good veins, rich in contents. There are so many deposits that it is indeed marvelous!" Samples of ore they brought back "assayed twenty marcs of silver per quintal (hundred-weight) of ore."

The Indians appeared to be friendly, so two padres were allowed to remain at Puaray Mission which they established, after they began their return south, but no sooner had they withdrawn than the Indians attacked the mission. The Chamuscado party was greatly outnumbered so they fled southward, leaving the two padres to their certain fate. The following year a new expedition which was to do more to open the northern borderlands to mining than any before was organized to learn the fate of the two priests. Their mission was also to explore northward to Teguayo, and if possible locate mines of gold and silver there. The expedition was small, having only 14 soldiers to guard it, and was organized by Fray Bernardino Beltran. It would be better known to history as the Espejo expedition, named for its co-leader, Don Antonio Espejo, a wealthy mine owner from Santa Barbara.

Espejo's stated purpose was to find mines richer than he already owned, but he would be remembered more for other things, for it was he who officially gave the name of New Mexico to New Spain's northern frontier. He also named the well worn trail which led to the northern mines, the Old Spanish Trail. A partial description of their route north read, "Northward beyond Sonora may be found other barbarous peoples, including the Apaches. Even further north are other nations such as the Zunis and Navajos, and beyond is New Mexico and the Utes." Clearly, even then New Mexico included the lands beyond the San Juan and Colorado Rivers, which included the Rocky Mountains and Great Basin. At Puaray Mission along the way, Fray Beltran verified the deaths of the two padres left behind by Fray Rodriguez, after which all of their efforts were directed to reaching Teguayo and the mines there. Fray Beltran later reported visiting and converting Indians at 74 Indian villages along the way, and estimated their population at 250,000.

At one of the villages as they proceeded northward they met the three guides left behind by Coronado forty-one years before. During those long years Andres, Gaspar and Anton had married

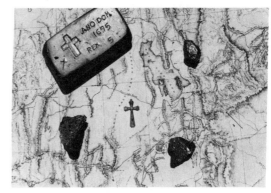

Even the earliest maps showed the Great Salt Lake and the riches in gold and silver to be found in that land, then called Teguayo.

and raised families. They had also learned a great deal about the lands beyond their villages. They told Espejo, "Far to the north and west there was a great lake named Copalla, where there were many towns inhabited by people who wore golden bracelets and ear-rings. It was the same land Coronado had sought, and to reach it required a journey of many leagues, as much as 60 days travel across a land where there was no water." In those days a league was reckoned as being 5,000 steps, or about 3.45 miles, but as Espejo was to learn, to travel a league in the wilderness of the canyonlands might take anywhere from an hour to a week to complete. The league varied greatly, only two centuries later it was the equivalent to 2.63 miles.

The Espejo quest was highly successful in locating rich mines. From Tusayan, which Pedro de Tovar had reached in 1540, Zuni Indians directed Espejo even further west, where after a long journey in which he detoured from the main travelled trail to the north, he located the rich silver and copper deposits which 300 years later would become the famous United Verde Mine of Jerome, Arizona. And near where Prescott was later settled by Arizona pioneers, Indians showed him another place where they had mined for silver. Espejo recorded, "I found their mines and with my own hands I dug ore from them, said by those who know such things to be very rich and to contain much silver." Returning to what he called "the old Spanish trail," Espejo travelled even further north where he discovered turquoise mines which had been worked from ancient times.

Several early accounts describe Indian mines which had been worked for turquoise or gold and silver from antiquity. The extent of the Indian mines discovered by Espejo and his contemporaries were as great as those later found at the so-called Spanish Diggings in Wyoming, which will be mentioned at length later. One surviving description of the Indian mines at Chalchihuite states: "I was astonished at the extent of their excavations. One pit is 200' in depth and 300' or more in width. It is no doubt very old, for at the bottom pine trees more than 100 years old are growing. This great excavation is made in solid rock, where tens of thousands of tons of rock have been broken out."

The records of Espejo's expedition mentioned another Indian mine he found. "It is excavated so deeply that chicken ladders (tree trunks with steps cut into them) are used to reach their depths. Natives have dug them for turquoise and for pigments of blue, green and brown colors, which they highly prize." Several of the mines he found may have been the same ones Coronado reported in 1540. But it was further north along the Old Spanish Trail that he made his greatest discovery, a mine which would keep the king's coffers filled with silver for more than a century, the fabulous El Mina del Tiro, the mine of the shaft.

Espejo was amazed at how extensive the workings at El Mina del Tiro were. The shaft appeared to be very old even then, and also very dangerous to enter, the workings simply following the ore veins down into the earth as they turned and twisted. Where the veins pinched together, a small "coyote hole" had been dug, only large enough to allow a worker to wiggle through. Indians carried heavy loads of ore in "zurrones," animal skin packs which had openings to put their arms through and with a strap across the forehead to bear part of the weight. They climbed out of the dangerous depths on chicken ladders braced against the sides of the shaft, and used burning cactus stalks which had animal tallow pounded into them for light. Espejo lost no time putting mining at El Mina del Tiro under the supervision of his padres. Records reveal that the ancient mine was still being worked 100 years later, and during that time thousands of Indians were killed or died in its depths. Yet as will be seen later, its location was concealed during an Indian revolt, and it has become one of the most famous of all lost mines.

After return of the Espejo party to Chihuahua, there was great excitement caused by the reports he made and the pack train of bullion bars he brought back. His journeys on the Old Spanish Trail north aroused such great interest in New Mexico that several new groups were quickly organized. Espejo reported that New Mexico was fertile and productive as well as being rich in mines. "It is as good a land as Coronado's men said it was, and with the discovery of good mines there, it is the best land every discovered. The mines are there, for I have brought back ores from them to prove their worth." And somewhere beyond the mines was the great lake surrounded by towns inhabited by people who wore golden bracelets!

Most of the small groups of prospectors hurrying northward were not licensed by the Governor, and were therefore illegal. Bans on trade or commerce with the Utes and the Commanches (The Spaniards considered any tribe not Zuni, Ute, Apache or Navajo as Commanches) had been proclaimed to protect the King's Quinto, as well as the secret tribute paid to the Governor and Viceroy. In 1590 the leaders of two mining parties were arrested on their return from the northern mines and all of the bullion they brought back with them confiscated. Gaspar Castano de Sosa with a party of miners had made an illegal journey to the north, where they destroyed 33 Indian villages and captured many Indians as slaves to work in their mines. On their return they were arrested. Also in 1590, Luis de Carabajal and his miners were arrested for opening mines in the north. Carabajal was charged with Judaism and later died in prison. His greatest offense against the crown was that he had tried to slip back into Chihuahua without paying the Royal Fifth on his treasure.

An especially interesting tale of illegal miners who went north to Teguayo in 1593 was one under the leadership of Juan Humana and Francisco Bonilla. The miners travelled northward through present Colorado, where it is believed they turned westward to explore the mountains of northern Utah, after which they continued northeast into Wyoming. A fight erupted over leadership of the party and Humana killed Bonilla. A priest accompanying the miners refused to follow a murderer and returned to Taos, where he reported the murder and that Humana had not followed the Viceroy's orders against entering the land of the Utes. Meanwhile Humana and his miners somehow obtained a great deal of gold somewhere in those northern mountains, said to be in the Uintas some 200 leagues northwest of Taos. They were travelling south through Colorado when they were attacked and massacred by Indians.

Soldiers sent out on the priest's complaint later discovered the massacre site, where because no Catholic Priest had been with the party, all had died without the last rites of the Church, their souls forever doomed to purgatory. The river canyon where they had died was named El Rio de los Animas Perdilos en Purgatorio, the river of lost souls in purgatory, today the Purgatoire River of

Colorado. The hoard of gold bullion their pack animals carried was not found, for it was either buried by the miners before they were killed or later hidden by the Indians. In 1884 the site was investigated by archaeologists from Bethany College. They found the skeletons and armor of Humana's miners, but no sign of their golden treasure. It is still there, somewhere.

If Espejo ignited the spark of interest in the mines of Teguayo, it was Juan de Onate who did the most to send exploring parties throughout that fabled land. Espejo had already petitioned the king for permission to explore Teguayo, at his own expense in exchange for a title of nobility, the right to make Encomiendas (slaves) of the Indians, exemption from taxes and a trade monopoly. Apparently the king thought Espejo's demands too excessive, for he awarded exclusive exploration rights to Don Juan de Onate, a wealthy mine owner. Onate agreed to pay the entire cost of his expedition, for he was the son of Christobal de Onate, owner of the fabulous Zacateras Mine, and was already wealthy in his own right. Onate agreed to pay all of the soldier's salaries, but noted that the king would be expected to pay for "six cannons, two dozen coats of mail and two dozen harquebuses, none of which are available here, as well as the wages of six Friars and the cost of six bells of the usual size, and all else that the new churchs to be built might require."

Onate's personal trappings included twelve suits of armor and twelve saddles, including one of blue and gold velvet with silver mountings and one of green and gold velvet, as well as one of crimson and black and two each of ocelot skins. Onate also promised to search for Humana and Bonilla, "So

Not every miner who found gold in the north lived to tell about it!

that they might be arrested and receive punishment for having entered illegally and contrary to the special prohibition of Your Majesty." Apparently Onate was unaware that Humana had already killed Bonilla or that the entire party had been slaughtered by Indians on the Purgatoire River.

It took three years for Onate's commission as Governor of New Mexico to come from Spain and two years more to assemble his great expedition. On January 26th, 1598, Onate led 130 soldiers, eight priests and a small band of Indian servants into the north on the Old Spanish Trail. Also taken were 83 carettas (wagons) and a herd of 7,000 cattle. Captain Perez de Villagia kept a daily journal of their travels in his Historia de la Nueva Mexico. Onate was to receive a salary of 6,000 gold ducats and would only be expected to pay one-half of the usual one-fifth of all treasure found. Many of his soldiers had their families with them, for Onate intended to establish colonies and missions along the way. He also expected to locate good ore veins and minerals, but he discovered that many mining parties had preceded him in secrecy, for he found many places where surface ore bodies and placer diggings had already been worked. Near present Salida, Colorado, he saw many places where extensive Spanish placer mining had been engaged in, apparently worked by illegal parties.

Near the present day "four corners" where Utah, Colorado, Arizona and New Mexico meet, at the forks of the Chama and Rio Grande Rivers, Onate established San Gabriel Mission and a settlement named San Juan de los Caballeros. From there he dispatched Captain Marcos Farfan to search for mines. The Captain was successful beyond their most hopeful expectations, as was described by Onate. "Six Indians from ranches in the mountains joined Captain Farfan and the next morning they took him up to a mine which was at a great height, although they could go up to it by horseback because the Indians had opened up a road. There they found a shaft three estados in depth (one estado being the height of a man), from which the Indians extracted ores for their adornment and for the coloring of their blankets, because in the mine there were brown, black, blue and green ores. The blue is so blue that it is understood that some of it is enamel (turquoise). I have been told that the silver there is the best in the

world. The mine also has a very large dump where there are also many good ores."

Many explorers observed the Indians' lack of interest in gold and silver except for ornamentation. "Silver is of no interest to them except for personal adornment. They grind it with other brightly colored stones and mix it into a paste for painting their faces and bodies. Silver here was first discovered by observing its use by the Indians. It is extracted from ores by the use of azoque (quicksilver) or by melting it in carboneras (furnaces) with charcoal. God in his great judgment must have given the Indians this silver so that it might be the means of attracting Christians here."

Assays of the ore found by Captain Farfan revealed that it contained 11 ounces of gold and silver per quintal, or 220 ounces to the ton. Captain Farfan immediately began mining, using genizaros (Indians earlier acquired and living more or less in the Spanish fashion) as foremen and captured Utes as laborers. Captain Farfan proved to be a hard task-master, his Indians treated as described by Agricola in De Re Metallica. "The earth, which is of the hardest rock, but full of gold and silver, is softened by putting fire to it. They follow the veins with only a torch to light the perfect darkness, their bodies sometimes appearing one color and sometimes another, according to the nature of the rocks. They throw the broken stones behind them, where small boys with great labor gather them up and carry them from the mine, where other workers break them into small pieces with hammers. An overseer shows how he would have it done. Those who are older or stronger then pound the pieces in a mortar until they are as small as a vetch.

"At length the masters of the work take the stones ground to powder and carry it away to perfect it. They spread the mineral so ground on a sloping board where they pour water over it and cleanse it, so that the lighter part of it is washed away and the heavier part which is gold remains behind because of its weight. Other workmen then take it away to where it is put into a midden (shallow pot), where it is mixed with a little lead, some grains of salt, a little tin and some barley bran. The midden is covered over with clay and put in a carbonera where it cooks for five days and nights. Then, when it is cooled, nothing is found in the pot but pure gold. And thus the gold is prepared with many great labors and difficulties."

Cargas, pack trains carrying silver bullion from the mountains, were sent along the Old Spanish Trail to the gulf coast. Each pack animal carried six bars of bullion, three on each side of the pack saddle. Each bar was approximately 4" thick and 24" to 30" long. The pack loads were not large, but they were very heavy, all that an animal could carry. Some recent reminders of the mines worked by Captain Farfan came to light in 1966 when the remains of an old smelter built of stone and adobe was discovered in the four corners area. Pieces of sixteenth century type tools were dug from the ruins, dating back to the Onate period.

Records at the Archives of the Indies reveal that soon after Captain Farfan began mining, 35 million pieces of gold and silver were shipped to Spain. Much of it came from mines like those discovered by Onate and the El Mine del Tiro discovered by Espejo, as well as from others worked by unknown miners, both legal and illegal, in the land of the Yutahs. Meanwhile Onate was exploring even further afield for even richer mines. He captured a Piute Indian who spoke "Ute-Aztecan," and from him learned "The source of the Rio Tizon (Colorado) is far to the north, where it flows from a great lake." The prisoner also told Onate a tantalizing tale of Sierra Azul, "a blue mountain of silver, north of the Rio Tizon, in Teguayo, near the lake called Copalla."

Taking 80 of his soldiers and two priests, Onate explored 200 leagues further north along the Old Spanish Trail leading into the Great Basin, where many more Indians were captured to work in Captain Farfan's mine. Onate engaged the Utes in a great battle in which he lost 13 of his men, including Captain Juan de Zoldivar, but his soldiers killed 700 Indians and took 600 more as prisoners. In a bloody act of revenge for the loss of his troops, Onate sentenced all male Indians over the age of 25 years to have one foot cut off and to give the king 25 years of service. All children from 12 to 25 years of age were sentenced to give 20 years of service. Two Indians from a neighboring nation to the north had their right hands cut off and were sent back to their people as a warning not to interfere with or ever attempt to fight the Spanish again. In addition, he had two chiefs hanged and their villages burned. Captain Villagia recorded in his "Historia" that Onate accomplished their punishment "in a tactful and gentle way."

Not only was Onate exceedingly cruel to the Indians, ordering hundreds of them killed, he was little better to his own soldiers. Angry at a Captain Aguilar, Onate murdered him by "thrusting a sword through his body, giving him no chance to confess, although he begged to do so, for he was in a state of sin." Captain Alonzo Albornaz was also murdered, "his body buried under stones where none dared look for it." Not long afterwards Onate received a message that he was to return to New Spain immediately. It was probably while on his return that he inscribed his name on Morro Rock as many others had before him. It can still be read, and states, "Juan de Onate passed by here the 16th of April, 1605." .

Upon his return to New Spain, Onate learned that he had been removed as Governor at the King's orders, for his extreme cruelty to the Indians. Nothing was mentioned about his cruelty to his own men. He was sent to Spain, "Forever exiled from New Mexico," and was ordered to pay a fine of 6,000 ducats. Onate appealed his conviction, and finally, in 1624, at age 75, he was pardoned and given a title of Inspector of Mines And Lodes. He never returned to New Spain.

CHAPTER SEVEN

EXPLORING THE GREAT BASIN

"Shadow, where can it be,
This land of El Dorado?
Over the mountains of the moon,
Down the valley of the shadow,
Ride, boldly ride,
If you seek for El Dorado!"

—Edgar Allen Poe

The first years of the seventeenth century were golden years for the Spanish Crown. Countless mines in the mountain west of New Mexico were sending millions in gold and silver to galleons along the gulf coast which carried the treasure to Seville. Many were illegal mines in the land of the Yutahs. The Old Spanish Trail from the mines was worn deep into the sandstone rock of the desert, so deeply that it can still be seen at places between the San Rafael River and the Sinbad Desert and between the Henry Mountains and the Spanish Bottoms on the Colorado River. Plate fleets with holds bulging with precious metals plundered from the Indians sailed for Spain, but not all reached their destination. Records reveal that of the hundreds of galleons which set sail, at least one in ten was lost to pirates or tropical storms.

Four treasure ships were lost in 1605, eight in 1628 and 13 more in 1641. In 1622 nearly every ship of the 28 galleons which sailed carrying $50,000,000 went to the bottom in a hurricane off the coast of Florida. The entire plate fleets of 1641 and 1715 were lost, but even with such terrible losses it is still estimated that during the first half of the seventeenth century more than one billion dollars in treasure arrived at Seville from the mines of the new world, at that time exceeding the entire money supply of Europe!

The first mint in the Americas was established at Mexico City in 1536, and after that date part of the gold and silver shipped to Spain was in minted coins. All of the gold and silver minted into coins was subject to the Quinto, and were marked to show that the Royal Fifth had been paid. Bullion bars were stamped with their weight, purity and a mark to show the king's tax had been paid. Most early coins minted at Mexico City were of silver, gold generally being cast into ingots. No coins minted before 1607 have been found, indicating they were undated before then. For several years copper coins were minted, but in a land rich in precious metals they were not accepted and were soon discontinued. The famous pieces of eight were minted after 1572.

Pieces of eight were also called "cobs," from the Spanish "Cabo de barra," meaning cut from a bar. Cobs were made by cutting planchetts from the end of a crudely cast bar of bullion. At the northern mines nothing more was required to produce a coin, but at the mint, the pieces were trimmed or clipped to the required weight, then heated and hand stamped or hammered between prepared dies. The coin produced was called a reale, and were of either gold or silver in 8, 4, 2, 1 and ½ reale size. A silver reale contained 3.5 grams of silver and was approximately 4 centimeters in diameter. Two crossing lines on the coins formed nine squares, each of which had an identifying symbol. The three squares of the top row revealed the mint, denomination and the minter's initial. The three center squares contained the letters P V A, Latin for "Plus Ultra," or "more beyond." Squares 7, 8 and 9 were the last three digits of the mint date, such as 671 for the year 1671. The reverse side of the coin showed a Catholic cross and the word "Hispania." Cobs, or pieces of eight, were the standard currency of the new world until well after the American Revolution of 1776.

Most of the treasure obtained from the new world was accumulated very quickly for several reasons. Most of the mines first worked were shallow, shafts seldom being more than 100' deep, usually in rich oxidized ore from which the gold or silver could easily be separated by the crude methods then used. During the first century of Spanish occupation, miners had an unlimited supply of free slave labor to work their mines. Also, over the centuries the Indians had acquired a great quantity of artifacts, which the Spaniards quickly acquired by trade or theft. The Indians did not place a monetary value on their artifacts, but considered them of value only as items of trade. "These things were not valued as treasure because buying and selling with gold and silver was unknown. Such objects were prized only for their beauty or splendor, to adorn themselves or their buildings, and since these objects were not necessary for their existence, they did not acquire them unless they had no other work to occupy their time. Yet as they saw that these metals were used to adorn places they valued highly, they employed their spare time seeking for them, to present to the sun, who was their God."

Exploration into the Great Basin regions reached a high point during the first half of the seventeenth century. One of the most daring adventurers, but today probably one of the least known, was Father Geronimo Zarate Salmeron. His journals describe mines north from Taos along the Old Spanish Trail far into the northern mountains. His were among the earliest descriptions of present day Utah and the Ute Indians, and it was he who gave the Wasatch Mountains of northern Utah their name. He made several journeys into the land of the Yutahs, in 1621 and again in 1624. He called the Indians Guasvatas, naming them for the high mountains where they lived. In his "Relacion" he described those Indians as being of the Guasvatas Nation, and noted that they spoke the Shoshonian language. The interpretation of his "Relacion" corrupted his written Guasvatas to the phoenetic Wasatch.

Father Salmeron wrote that the great lake where the Guasvatas Indians lived was called by them Laguna del Oro, or the Lake of Gold. They told him that it was long sought after Lake of Copalla, the ancient home of the Aztecs. On his sketch maps, Lake Copalla is shown as Laguna del Oro. He placed it as being "fourteen days journey beyond the Tizon River, or 400 leagues from the northern settlements and 540 leagues from Mexico." Also interesting is the fact that the Guasvatas Indians told him of other Yutahs living

even beyond Copalla, who at that early date were already using Spanish words in their language.

In 1626 Father Salmeron described the mines in the lands of the Guasvatas. "There are silver, copper, lead and lodestone, as well as garnet deposits. In all those ranges there is nothing but deposits, where I discovered many and filed on them for His Majesty. I took 18 arrobas of ore (450 pounds) and distributed those ores at all the mining camps I passed through in order that all might see them. Before all things there are mineral deposits, and there is no corner which has them not!" Note that he used the term "mining camps," quite possibly the first use of that term which we generally attribute to writers of modern times. And since he described the mines, there must have been such places in the mountains of Ute country. That Spanish frontiersmen mingled freely with the northern Utes is further evidenced by reports of French fur trappers that many Utes had obtained Spanish horses by 1630, and that a brisk trade in horses existed as far north as Montana soon afterwards.

Among the first to describe the Indians and mines of Ute country was Father Estevan de Perea, who in June, 1604, with Fray Bartolome Romero and Fray Francisco Muniz explored far into the Great Basin provinces. Theirs was a legal expedition, the party being accompanied by Governor Francisco de Silva Nieto, as well as "thirty well armed soldiers." Their purpose was to search for mines of gold, but the few records of this expedition still intact are too meager in detail to reveal their course of travel exactly, however, the Perea expedition was among the first authorized civil-church parties to explore Ute country for mines.

At about the same time Salmeron and Perea were exploring the northern borderlands, Father Alonso Benavides wrote an account of his travels from 1625 to 1629. In 1630 he recorded that he had found "A very great treasure of mines, very rich and prosperous in both gold and silver, as well as deposits of very fine garnets." Exactly where his trails led is now unknown, but it is interesting to note that "fine garnets" are found in few places south of present day Montana. While en route to the northern mines Father Benavides mentioned passing by turquoise mines, as well as "mines of alum, which is used by the natives to dye their cloth." Turquoise, long prized by the Indians, was also a gem much coveted by the Spaniards. In his journals Governor Mendoza wrote that he presented to Cortez "four turquoise which are said to be worth more than a load of gold!"

A forgotten and now almost unknown expedition of 1618 into the far north was that of Vincent de Saldivar, the notice of which was recorded in 1664. In that year Father Nicholas de Freyta of the Franciscan Order of Strict Observance wrote an account of Governor Diego Penalosa's journey to Quivira in the year 1662. Of pertinent interest here, however, is an addition to that document, titled "An account of a previous expedition." Father Freytas noted that the account "was copied faithfully and literally from the original." It begins as follows:

"In the year 1618 the Maestre de Campo, Vincent de Saldivar, set out on an expidition of discovery with 47 soldiers well equipped, accompanied by Father Friar Lazarus Ximenez, of the Order of St. Francis." Father Freytas's account relates that the expedition passed through the land of the Moquis and "marched through uninhabited parts for fifteen days more." They journeyed through a "land of fire" to near the lands of French Aca-nada (Canada), only by good fortune passing undetected through a land where Indians warned them there lived "A terrible nation of giants, so huge that one of our men on horseback was small compared to them."

Happily Saldivar's men never encountered any giants, even though they travelled far into the north. Apparently they prepared maps of Teguayo, "As clearly drawn as we could," however, no copy is known to exist unless it is hidden or lost somewhere in the mass of files at Seville. It is unlikely they will be found, for Father Freytas noted, "The memorials of Vincent de Saldivar are extremely rare, for they were not written for the public, but only for the use of high personages."

The numerous expeditions seeking mines in the north captured many Indians to be used as slaves at those mines. It was especially easy to capture the primitive "Diggers" and "Gosh-Utes" during the early spring when they were weak from starvation. The mountain Utes were not so easily taken, as was noted by Father Alonzo Posada, who wrote: "Utes have great courage and are great fighters, they are equal to the Apaches and are never known to turn their backs in combat. They do not retreat, they either win or die!"

By Royal Decree, the minimum age at which Indians could be legally enslaved was age ten for boys and age nine for girls, both of whom could be held in bondage until age 20. They could be worked after that age, however, if the padre believed it was necessary to keep them from sin or for the sake of the faith. Since many padres had interests in the mines, they usually found it necessary to keep their Indians occupied with worthwhile work beyond age 20. Although several Spanish monarchs and most Roman Popes had denounced slavery, still it flourished throughout every region of the new world. A history of the Northern Utes records that as early as 1638 some 80 Utes were captured by Spanish soldiers and were taken to Santa Fe where they were sold as slaves. They were sold for 200 to 300 pesos each.

But the situation of Indian women may have improved slightly, for by a new decree the king had ordered, "No pregnant woman after the fourth month shall be sent to the mines, or made to plant hilloks, but shall be used only in household tasks, such as cooking and weeding." It was a very considerate gesture by the King.

The period of the 1650s saw many mines opened throughout the mountains, so many that King Philip IV issued a new law which prohibited governors of the northern territories from engaging in mining. Apparently the king believed that if the governors had no interest in the mines, they would be more diligent in collecting his Royal Fifth, but his hope was in vain, for his order was ignored while the mine owners, governors and viceroy grew even richer. One of the richest mines was El Mina del Tiro, discovered by Espejo in 1580 and still producing a fortune in silver and gold a century later. During the 1660s El Mina del Tiro was owned by Governor Don Joachim y Robal.

Indians forced to work in El Mina del Tiro were treated no better than they had been in Espejo's time. The mine had been dug deep into the rocky depths with a vertical shaft until water was encountered, after which countless Indians were employed carrying animal skin bags of water to the surface, but they could only check the flow, not lower it. All along the tunnel leading from the shaft, water carriers stood by torch light, day and night steadily baling water or passing water bags from hand to hand. Many of the mine's richest ore bodies were later excavated by horizontal tunnels when the water level could not be lowered further.

In an early account a padre sympathized with the Indian's sad plight. "There we saw many Indians laboring in the mines. The soldiers are sometimes harsh in their treatment of the Indians, neither is it strange then for the Indians to flee from the Spaniards to escape laboring in the mines. Liberty means much to these primitive people, who have always known libery." Many of those who did escape took Spanish horses with them, and sometimes even swords or other arms. Old records frequently tell of parties being sent into the far reaches of Ute country to capture runaway slaves. In 1664 the Governor sent Juan de Archuletta with a troop of soldiers to pursue runaway slaves. They pursued the runaways north through Colorado and into Wyoming. He was able to recover most of the slaves, but his scant records do not reveal his exact route; however, we know that he visited the so-called Spanish Diggings in present Niobrara County. The "diggings" aren't Spanish at all, but are ancient Indian mines, dating back 6,000 years. There on the plains countless thousands of Indians over hundreds of years dug jasper and agate to be fashioned into arrow heads and spear points. They were traded with other Indians as far away as the gulf coast. The diggings there are almost unbelievable in size, consisting of countless pits as much as 30 feet deep and as large as 50 acres in size, covering more than 400 square miles! The extent of their excavations, dug only with stone tools, staggers the imagination even today.

CHAPTER EIGHT

THE SPANISH MISSIONS

"Bell, book and candle
shall not drive me back,
When gold and silver
becks me to come on!"

— William Shakespeare

Juan de Onate was not the first to establish missions along the Old Spanish Trail leading into the Great Basin. The Rodriguez-Archuletta expedition built Puaray Mission in 1565 and there are references to other missions built in the north as early as 1574. In 1644 Padre Perez de Ribas, Padre Provincial of the Company of Jesus, the Jesuits, described in his Triumphs Of Our Saintly Faith Among Peoples The Most Barbarous Of The New Orb, some of the workings of the mission system, which he stated was started soon after the first conquistadores arrived in the new world. "Since the inception of the mission system there have been built more than fifty missions, at which there have been baptized in the Holy Waters some 300,000 souls."

By Royal Order, the king had directed that at each real of mines there must be a church, although many of the early missions established at isolated mines and rancherias were at first only crude places. Many were little more than boweries, but most were built of adobe mud, which has long since melted away so that now no trace of them remains, except perhaps for an outline on the ground. Sometimes stone foundations can still be seen under the brush.

The usual method of establishing a mission in the north at a lone mine or real of mines was the building of a rough hut or cabin, to which the padres attracted the Indians by displaying pictures, something the Indians had never seen. A few trinkets or pieces of cloth and some colorful banners also enticed them. A small statue of the Virgin prevailed upon the Indians' already superstitious nature. Gifts of food induced familiarity, and the padre's worldly knowledge gave him great status with the natives. By demonstrating the advantages of growing crops or building shelters increased his stature. From there it was but a short step to baptism, which the Indian probably never understood, and thence to working at the mission fields or at the padre's mine. Unfortunately, the cost of civilization was high, and the treatment received at the hands of the Jesuits became too oppressive, so much so that eventually the Indians rose in revolt.

Where the Indian population was not a roving one, as it was in the northern mountains, more permanent and beautiful missions could be built. Following is one example of how this was accomplished:

"The Indians' interest soon led them to the construction of permanent churches. There were priests who could teach them to make adobes, fit stones or hew in the proper proportions great timbers. They entered into their labor with great enthusiasm. Sometimes a large number of Indians could be seen carrying one great timber. The women and children took part also. Finally there was completed a great church, which was dedicated with much feasting. Other Indians gazed upon this fine building and in their hearts was born a great desire to have a similar church."

Even though the much smaller missions of the Great Basin region were not so elaborate as the one described, nevertheless, it was the king's desire that all should be complete. The king ordered the Royal Treasury that each mission should have "Two complete sets of vestments for the priests, and adornments for the altars, also a set of bells and musical instruments." Many of the missions built in the northern mountains had bells cast at Ojo Del Espiritu Santo, the Spring of the Holy Ghost, which was located near Cuba, New Mexico, where there were mines whose ore contained a high content of silver and copper. Bullion from the ore was cast into mission bells, the silver giving them a beautiful mellow tone.

Padre Provincial de Ribas described one mission as being "Rich in ornaments, such as lamps and goblets of silver. Today it serves as a shrine for travellers through this once forbidden land." The great domed cathedrals further south often boasted "gilded altars so rich that a common price for one was twenty thousand gold ducats. Their altar cloths, candlesticks, hangings, jewels on the statues with crowns of gold and silver would amount to the worth of a silver mine."

By Royal Decree the purpose of the missions was to convert, to civilize and to exploit. In 1574 Lopez de Velasco, the Geographer of New Spain, reported there were estimated to be several thousand Indian towns with as many as five million inhabitants, all subject to conversion and paying tithing or tribute. By the same time there were already 200 Spanish towns, in addition to many small miniming camps, haciendas and stock ranches. In comparison to the Indian population, there were approximately 180,000 Spaniards and 40,000 Negro slaves. But even by that early date there were already 21 missions in New Spain and probably half again as many in New Mexico, then everything north of the Rio Grande River, or New Spain. By 1630 more than 25 missions had been established throughout New Mexico, where nearly 50 priests had converted an estimated 60,000 Indians to Catholicism. Most of the missions in the far north were only temporary at best, lasting only as long as the mines where they were located kept working. Many were only visitas, having no resident padre and visited only infrequently by an itinerant Jesuit Priest who carried with him his Bible, vestments and chalices to hold the wine of Holy Communion.

Although many of those northern missions have long since become forgotten and their sites now unknown, a few scant records still tell their story. In 1585 Father Augustine Rodriguez, of the Rodriguez-Archuletta expedition of 1565, with two priests named Marcos and Venabides led a party northwest from Taos to establish a mission, believed by some to be located at the famed Lost Josephine mine. In 1628 Father Bartolome Romero accompanied Governor Satedo and an escort of soldiers to the San Juan River where they built an adobe and log mission, but whether it was in Utah or Colorado is uncertain; however, it is of interest

that in 1971 a copper bell of the type used at such missions was found near the town of Blanding in southern Utah. The University of Utah dated it as being more than 500 years old, of Spanish origin, and of very fine craftsmanship.

In the far north only a set of bells and perhaps a crude altar was the padre's visita.

Research accomplished by Dr. Donald Moorman of Weber State College at Ogden, Utah, has uncovered much new information on heretofore unknown missions built as far north as the mountains bordering Utah and Wyoming. His and other research has revealed that some 14,000 Indians had been baptized at those northern missions by 1617. There were 43 small mountain missions by 1626 where some 34,000 Indians had been baptized, and by 1630 there had been 86,000 baptisms. To insure that the missions of the new world would have sufficient clergy, King Philip III instructed the Archbishop of Mexico, Don Juan de la Serna, to establish Jesuit colleges to train missionaries. They were built at Mexico City, San Luis de la Paz and at the northern mining camp of Zacatecas. Schools to train Indians in the ways of Catholicism were established at many missions throughout the northern mines. Most were built at the center camp of a real of mines.

It was very much to the advantage of the Jesuits to establish missions wherever they could, for the Royal Treasury paid each mission the equivalent of $450 each year, plus 350 pesos for each friar assigned. The Crown also paid an initial $1,000 for vestments, bells and tools. There were also private gifts and endowments, often greater than the crown paid. The king was expected to provide military protection if needed, which included the soldier's salaries. All missions were expected to become self-supporting, and the Royal Quinto was to be paid on all income, whether from mining or other sources. But rarely was the King's Fifth paid in full, for mission padres were also often mine owners, and were as reluctant as anyone else to let the king know the true extent of their wealth.

Padres who were mine owners, or at least operators of mines, as well as being the person charged with protecting the Indians, often inflicted the worst punishment on them. Many missions owned large herds of livestock; horses, sheep, cattle and hogs. Depending upon their location, many also had large cultivated fields with grape arbors for their wineries. But even the poorest mission in the most rugged mountains had to raise its own corn, squash and beans for sustenance, for there was no source from which supplies could be had. It was the Indian who worked in the mines, fields, shops, grist mills and wineries.

A Frenchman named La Perouse described conditions at missions he was allowed to visit. He wrote that the Indian's day was divided between labor and prayer. Any deviation from the tasks assigned by the padre brought instant punishment. He noted that he saw many Indians who had been cruelly beaten, some with their noses or hands cut off, some were in chains, and he often heard the crack of the whip being applied. La Perouse said that the padres told him that punishment was a suitable penance for the salvation of their souls. Indians were forced to do all of the work and in return received a daily ration of bread and broth. If one escaped and was brought back by soldiers, he was given fifty lashes. La Perouse concluded that because of the isolated locations of the missions, often 600 leagues or more from any permanent settlement, and the absolute authority of the padre,

combined with their zeal to convert Indians and save their souls, the mission system bred the worst possible kind of abuses.

An English Jesuit Priest who later left the order lamented that "At least three million Indians have been murdered by their Spanish masters." Conditions became so bad that Father Bartolome wrote in his last will and testament, "Surely God will wreak his fury and anger against Spain for the unjust wars waged against the Indians. Our Christians have let it be seen that in the Indies, their God is gold!" Many Jesuit Priests who were mine owners did not pay the Royal Fifth because they did not have to answer to civil law. In one celebrated case, one Father Valencia refused to pay the Quinto, and he was ordered to be arrested. He appealed to his Bishop, who ruled that civil officials had no authority to judge or fine a priest. Another priest was charged with causing the death of an Indian as the result of a severe whipping he received for not attending mass. The priest contended that the Indian had died of illness, which was the reason he didn't attend mass. The priest was transferred to another mission.

In another recorded case, a certain priest was accused of owning a number of unbranded Indians working at his mines. He countered that he had purchased the slaves from another mine owner, who was then dead and so could not testify, at which time they did not bear the king's brand. The priest was ordered to pay the usual tax on the slaves and see that they properly branded, but had to pay no other penalty. An even greater travesty occurred in a case where an Indian who was being whipped, attacked and killed his tormentor. The court decided that the slave had not acted in defense of his life, which had not been threatened, and condemned him to be hanged, with his right arm severed and placed on a pole as a warning to other Indians who might think to strike their master!

When the Indians witnessed the Spaniard's greed for gold, and saw that if necessary every Indian who was captured would be forced to work in the mines until they died, they not only hid their own gold and silver objects and denied any knowledge of such metals, they even went to great effort to conceal their own mines and hide all evidence of veins of ore from the Spaniards. At each mine and mission the Indians soon learned that to refuse the orders of the mine owner or padre quickly resulted in severe punishment or death. Medicine men who had great influence over their tribesmen skillfully planned revolts to overthrow their oppressors. Usually any attempt by the Indians to overcome their Spanish masters failed, but in 1616 the first organized revolt took the Spaniards by surprise, as was described as follows:

"With great intriques and enchantments this old hechicero (medicine man) warped the minds and souls of the Indians, and with his chiefs he plotted a simultanious uprising throughout the sierras, attacking at once the reals of mines and churchs in each place and driving awy the miners, padres and their Christian Indians. The attack was planned for the time of the Festival of the Virgin. A beautiful statue of the Virgin had been sent from Mexico City, and the Indians believed that all of the Spaniards would be away from their mines to .attend the festival, and would not be carrying arms during the celebration. The precise date for the attack was fixed for the 21st of November.

"By Friday, more than 500 Indians had gathered to join the attackers. They set fire to the entire settlement and made a fierce assault upon the church. The house of the padres they set on fire with burning arrows. When everything was going up in flames, an Indian named Michael, who the Spaniards trusted, shouted to the besieged that those wishing to escape could surrender with assurance their lives would be spared. There being no other recourse, they laid down their arms, and with their families gathered at a place near the church. The mission Padre carried in his arms the reliquary of the church while another carried an image of the Saintly Mother.

"They began speaking kindly to the savages, when suddenly a voice rose from the multitude, shouting that the God of the Christians was not their God. The Indians were put in a frenzy and began attacking the helpless prisoners. The images of our Holy Mother and of Our Saviour were trampled into the earth, and all of the Spaniards were murdered except for three who escaped. Their fury was then turned upon the Padre, who was seized while the savages in derision recited words from the Holy Scriptures which they had learned from him. Thus he was held exposed until an arrow pierced his body. Finally he was killed with a blow from an axe, but as he died he cried to his tormentors, 'Do as you will, I am in the hands of God!'

"On the day following, the savages attacked at the houses where some Spaniards had taken refuge. They soon opened some holes in the roof and walls and through these openings fired burning arrows. The defenders climbed to the roof, but finally they were compelled to surrender. No mercy was given, even worse, the savages exercised the most extreme cruelty on men, women and children while murdering them. Of 300 persons, only two escaped. Here also died some 600 faithful Christian Indians."

One can't help but note that any native who was a Christian or friendly to the Spaniards is referred to as an Indian, but the slaves who joined the revolt were called savages. Eventually the Spanish reconquered the sierras and reclaimed the mines there. Sixty Indians were identified as being among those participating in the revolt and were hanged from trees. "Except for a few stubborn ones, those who had taken part in the terrible rebellion were once more cultivating fields, working at the mines or rebuilding churches. The cost to the Royal Coffers of Spain was 800,000 pesos of eight reales each, without taking into account the lives lost, the mines and churches destroyed and the many souls lost to heaven." In the end nothing had really changed, for the Indians were soon enslaved again, but their memories were long, and the best planned revolt against the Spanish was yet to come.

CHAPTER NINE

THE OLD SPANISH TRAIL

"Something hidden. Go and find it.
Go and look beyond the ranges.
Something lost beyond the ranges,
Lost and waiting for you, Go!"

— Rudyard Kipling

The route northward from New Spain (Mexico) into the far reaches of the Great Basin of New Mexico was called the Spanish Trail by Espejo in 1581 and the Old Spanish Trail by Onate in 1604. With later expeditions of Salmeron, Perea, Romero, Benavidas, Posada and many others now forgotten or unknown, the old trail became a vital lifeline between the northern mines and missions and the outposts of Spanish civilization at places like Chama, Taos and Santa Fe. New Mexico's capital city was moved from Onate's San Gabriel Mission to Santa Fe in 1610, but Santa Fe had become an important trade center long before that, and with the move of government there it became the jumping off place to follow the several forks of the old trail north. Contrary to some misconceptions, the Old Spanish Trail was not just a single track through the wilderness, for it had several main trails with many forks and side branches leading from it.

It is unknown who the first Spaniard to trod the old trail was, but many miners, traders, slaving parties and Catholic Priests seeking souls to save were following its tortuous route by the early 1600s. We know that prospectors sought the gold of Teguayo even before that, while Ute Indians were captured as slaves not far from the Great Salt Lake soon afterwards. One of the earliest accounts including one of the best descriptions of the old trail from Santa Fe to Utah Lake was written by Fray Alonzo de Posada in 1686 as part of a special report to the Council of the Indies to aid in a royal report being prepared on the riches of Teguayo as reported by Governor Diego Penalosa in 1664.

Fray Posada had served as a missionary in New Mexico from 1650 to 1660, much of that time "in the most remote parts of the province." During those years he had the additional duty as Cusdodia, or administrator of the Franciscan Order, which position gave him access to all records, including those pertaining to earlier Spanish expeditions into the far north. To acquaint the Council with the geography of New Mexico, Posada first described Teguayo and the route to it.

Posada described Teguayo as being those lands north of the Rio San Juan and west of the Rocky Mountains, while Quivira was located east of the Rockies. The trail north from Santa Fe passed by "a very high mountain called Sierra Blanca and beyond the Rio San Juan, into the land of the Yutas." The Yutas lived near "a great lake of salt at the end of the Long River," and were comprised of several nations. "It is not merely conjecture but certain that there are many people and diverse nations in the Kingdom of Teguayo." Fray Posada added that while a minister on that frontier he had an Indian guide called Juanillo who informed him that he had once been a prisoner at the Lake of Copalla, captured by a people who lived by the borders of a great lake and who spoke different languages.

From the Rio San Juan, "which runs straight west for 70 leagues and is possessed by the Navajo nation, the trail passes into the land of the Yutas, a warlike nation. Crossing through this nation for 60 leagues in the same northwest direction one comes to some hills, and travelling through that country for another 50 leagues, more or less, one arrives at the great lake in the land Indians of the north call Teguayo. The Mexicans call the lake Copalla, according to their ancient traditions the place where all Indians, even those of Mexico, Guatemala and Peru originated." Note that the journey of 110 leagues "more or less" northwest of the San Juan River would place the Spanish adventurers almost exactly at today's Utah Valley.

Fray Posada played down the quantity of gold at Teguayo as compared to Mexico, nevertheless he wrote "The nations who dwell there do what the Indians used to do in New Spain (Mexico), they clean gold and silver from the sands of the rivers. They wear earrings and have bracelets of gold, which they always wear on the left arm. Still, it is a fact that the Indians never did benefit from gold and silver until the Spanish came."

Fray Posada did not encourage settlement of Teguayo, saying that such isolated settlers could not expect aid "because they will be so far away from the Kingdoms peopled by Spaniards. Neither can wagons go there because of the difficulties of the land, cut by many raging rivers and rough mountains, and the length of the road, 500 leagues more or less, which must be crossed among infidel and barbarous enemy Indians. To settle those lands would require a great number of military escorts." But although official permission to settle Teguayo was withheld and prospectors and traders were forbidden to enter the lands of the Utes, only a token fine was levied against those who did so, the yearly fine amounting to little more than a license to trespass.

The old trail north from Santa Fe had many variations, such as those followed by slavers, each new trail being used only so long as a sufficient number of Indians could be captured in a particular area. But the routes which led to mining camps were more permanent, often being used for many years with only slight deviations. Many of the mines they led to were worked for many years, mines like El Mina del Tiro, the fabulous Pish-La-Ki and the famed Josephine de Martinique, as well as hundreds of others, many unnamed and now forgotten. The purpose of the trail was to supply isolated mines and missions in the far north and to convey pack trains of gold and silver from the mines in the mountains beyond Utah Valley to Santa Fe and down the Rio Grande or Rio Colorado of Texas to the gulf coast. It is along that main travelled trail that remants and reminders can best be found today.

From Santa Fe the trail went northward past the frontier outpost of Abique and followed the Chama River north to the forks of the Chama and Rio Grande, where Onate built his Mission San Gabriel. From there it turned more northwesterly across the southwest corner of Colorado to the San Juan River, where Father Romero built his log and adobe mission in 1628. For many years a variation of the trail continued north through Colorado, turning west either at present day Moab on the Colorado or further north near Vernal on the Green River. A century and a half later Father Rivera chose the Moab route while Father Escalante followed the more northerly trail.

A leading work on Colorado describes the trail through the western part of that state. "The Old Spanish Trail in Colorado had been used by the early Spaniards for exploring and mining in centuries past. Vast treasures were transported over the old trail, but not all of it got where it was intended to go; the Indians prevented that. They massacred the miners and appropriated their pack animals and merchandise for themselves. A few signs of those encounters are still to be seen, old bones of animals and men, arrow points and an occasional bit of rusted metal or an old spur as evidence of the battles fought there.

"Some have confused the Old Spanish Trail with the Escalante Trail of 1776, but the two are not the same. The course of the Old Spanish Trail lay north from Abique, up the Little Chama River, over the continental divide and across the San Juan River and its tributaries to the divide at the head of the Middle Fork of the Piedia River, about 50 miles northwest of Pagosa Hot Springs. Along the trail there is an unmistakeable landmark, La Ventana, a natural doorway some 200' high at the crest of the continental divide, 75 miles northwest of the hot springs. La Ventana is a permanent landmark used by all early Spanish travelers as an unmistakeable guide."

From Father Romero's mission on the San Juan, the main trail crossed the river into southern Utah. An important fork of the trail did not cross the San Juan, but instead continued west to Navajo Mountain and the famous Pish-La-Ki Mine, better known some 250 years later as the Merrick & Mitchell Mine, which will be discussed at length later. The trail continued to the Colorado River which it crossed at one of several places, but usually at the Spanish Bottoms, where steps hand cut into the sandstone walls for pack animals to follow can still be seen today. Beyond the Colorado another important fork in the trail was reached where a branch turned westward to the Henry Mountains and probably the most famous

The Old Spanish Trail heading west to Fish Lake and the Virgin River. *(A Charles Kelly photo.)*

Between South Temple Wash and the San Rafael River some two dozen or more grave mounds have been found, indicating a Christian burial site. Local Indian tradition tells of a battle between Utes and Spaniards which occurred in the long ago. Most of a party of 30 miners were killed, only a few escaping by hiding in the rocks. The Indians captured their pack animals and hid the loads of bullion they were carrying. To find the cache you will have to hike the rugged trail between Goblin Valley and the San Rafael Swell to find the grave site. According to the Indian legend, it is not far from there to where the bullion is cached.

At Coal Wash the trail led over shale ledges where even today it can be seen, worn as much as two feet deep into the sandstone rock. Several Catholic crosses and dates from the early 1700s can be found along Coal Wash. The trail continued into Price Valley, where it followed the Price River to the head of Spanish Fork Canyon and down Soldier Creek into Utah Valley, the Indian's Land of Teguayo. Two other branches of the trail already mentioned joined the main trail at Spanish Fork Canyon. The route from Moab on the

of all lost Spanish mines, the Josephine de Marinique. More about that well travelled trail and famous mine later.

The main trail continued to the northwest, where at the Dirty Devil River an infrequently used side trail turned to the west to the old mines near Fish Lake. Beyond there it continued west to the head of the Virgin River, which it followed to Las Vegas Springs and south to the missions built by Fathers Francisco Garces and Juan Bautista de Anza. It also led down the Gila River to the old Tumacacori Mission built by Father Eusebio Kino, located some 25 miles northwest of the present mission. The Las Vegas trail also crossed the desert to California and Mission San Gabrial, now Los Angeles and Mission Monterey. During the heyday of the fur trappers, this branch became the most heavily used section of the old trail.

Following the Dirty Devil River northward, the main trail crossed the Sinbad Desert to South Temple Wash, the Head of Sinbad and the San Rafael River, which it followed to Coal Wash.

Faded Catholic crosses with ancient dates still remain hidden along the old trail north in places like the Sinbad Desert and the San Rafael country.

Colorado crossed the Green River and continued west to the Price River, while the northern route from Vernal followed the Duchesne River to Strawberry Valley and turned down Diamond Fork Canyon to the Spanish Fork trail.

From Utah Valley several trails led into the surrounding mountains. The most used trail went up the Provo River Canyon, where it forked near present Heber City. The most used fork turned northeast to mines like the Mine of the Yutahs, the Josephine on Currant Creek, the Mine of Lost Souls and a group of others later known as the Lost Rhoades Mines. The northwest fork of the trail led to the Weber River and several mines in the Kamas-Hoyt Peak area, shown on even the earliest maps as "The Old Spanish Mines." Another trail led west from Utah Valley into the Tintic Mountains where many old mines were later located near the mining town of Eureka, and even further west to the barren ranges of the Great Salt Lake Desert. At the western edge of the desert there is a rocky crag called Montezuma Peak. When the first American miners prospected its barren slopes they discovered old mine workings, where they dug gold at camps they named Clifton and Gold Hill. Another trail went north past the Great Salt Lake, where Mormon pioneers discovered stone ruins and evidence of mining, and continued into the far north of Idaho and Wyoming. The further north the old trail was followed, the dimmer it became.

A few men have spent their lifetimes tracing the Old Spanish Trail and locating the lost mines and historic places along it. Among them were such dedicated researchers as Edgar T. Wolverton, Frank Silvey, Burt Silliman and Charles Kelly. We are indebted to them for their research, which was not of the "armchair" variety, but came from years spent in the deserts and mountains and in hundreds of lonely camps along the trail. Edgar T. Wolverton was an accomplished miner and engineer who spent most of his life tracing the old trails and seeking the Lost Josephine Mine of the Henry Mountains. He found many old Spanish diggings there and traced the Orejas Des Oso, the Bear's Ears Trail, that fork leading from the Colorado River into the Henry Mountains.

Wolverton traced the Orejas Des Oso Trail from Monument Valley into the Abajo Mountains, to where it crossed Bear's Ears Pass, which land-mark gave it its name. From the pass it wound its way down to the Colorado River which it crossed at the Spanish Bottoms. Wolverton found the stone steps cut into the canyon wall so pack animals could climb its near vertical sides. He located several places where animals had fallen to their death, where nothing remained except pieces of bone, fragments of ancient leather packs and small piles of gold ore that had scattered where they fell. He mentioned that he could follow the old trail simply by following the pieces of ore which had been dropped from packs in the long ago.

Wolverton discovered the ruins of visitas, which he called "way stations" a few days apart from each other, and wrote: "The way stations were part of a chain of rest missions which extended from northwest New Mexico to the Green River. We followed the old trail at places where it was worn several feet into the solid sandstone. Near the northwest end of the Abajo Mountains we found an extensive burial ground." Whether or not this was another place where Spanish miners were attacked and killed isn't yet known, but if it is, there could be a bullion cache hidden somewhere nearby. It might be a good place for someone to check out with a metal detector. Wolverton added that the trail into the Henry Mountains "required definite and intelligent planning and improvements," being graded at places and with stone walls still intact along the steep mountain sides.

Burt Silliman also spent many years tracing sections of the old trail, and in a letter to well known historian Leroy Hafen, he wrote: "The evidence accumulates that with a lot of free Indian labor, a great deal of trail building and mining was done. The physical evidence of old mines with trees 200 years old growing in their workings, as well as the Indian tradition of slavery in the mines, all strongly suggest that the old trail is as much as 300 years old. The more I investigate the more evidence accumulates. I'm sure that to a historian this is heresy, an opinion in conflict with the authorities, but nevertheless, the evidence continues to accumulate!"

Frank Silvey, who spent many years following and studying the old trail and the ancient names and dates along it, described those sections of the trail in the Kamas Valley and Weber River area in the same terms. Charles Kelly, investigator, explorer, national park superintendent, and dean of the Utah historians wrote: "I now realize that Spanish mining expeditions penetrated a lot of country that we have no record of. Spanish mining tools were found in Millard County where later good gold placers were located, and an ancient Spanish arrastra was found near Marysvale. All on the Old Spanish Trail that we know so little of."

With the Old Spanish Trail well established, the northern mountains experienced a flood of adventurers who left mysteries which have never been solved. A very few expeditions left detailed records, but most left only cryptic waybills and mysterious maps to record their passing. Others inscribed strange signs and markings on trees or stone ledges to mystify those who find them today. There are Spanish inscriptions dated 1640 and 1642 on sheer stone walls in Glen Canyon which have never been explained. Why they were placed there or what their significance is, is unknown; however, Shivwit Indians who once made their home at the mouth of the Virgin River on the Colorado told the early pioneers that their fathers had once been forced to work in Spanish mines near there. A long time afterwards several discoveries made nearby strongly supports the Indian tradition.

In 1911 a gold placer was discovered at the confluence of the Virgin and the Colorado, where miners recovered nuggets heavily coated with quicksilver. Since there are no natural quicksilver deposits anywhere along the Virgin, a conclusion was made that the nuggets had been lost from some earlier mining activity, probably from an old arrastra. Not long afterwards the ruins of an arrastra was found higher up along the river! In 1973 professional treasure hunter Gene Ballinger reported that a cache of some 600 Spanish church books, ledgers and journals had been found in a leather chest where they had been hidden in a cave along the Virgin a very long time before. The books reportedly were from a Jesuit mission library. Finding old book caches is not all that unusual. Occasional reports still surface of old maps and waybills which have survived the ravages

The mysterious 1642 inscription at Glen Canyon. Who made it? *(Courtesy Utah State Historical Society.)*

of time being found in secret places at old missions and mines.

Another Utah cache containing Spanish documents and hand written books was found in a shallow cave by a family on a weekend outing in 1975. They had been searching for Chinese opium bottles along the old Central Pacific grade near the north end of the Great Salt Lake when the find was made. Another large chest of old church and mine records hidden in a cave in the Ladrone Mountains of New Mexico by Fray Diego Jimenz during the 1680 revolt was found in 1916. They dated back to 1531! The records pertained in part to the rich Mina Nuestra Senora de los Reyes de Lineras of those mountains. It had been concealed by Indians in 1680 but was relocated in 1713. The chest of ancient records were in a cave close by the mine, still they were not found until 200 years later.

To those "armchair historians" the Old Spanish Trail is just a fable, something they can't believe is real because there is no documented proof that it existed. But they overlook the real proof, the old well-worn trail itself. And they ignore the crumbling ruins of missions that mark the long miles that it snakes its way across deserts and mountains, and the ancient names, dates and treasure signs left along the way. Nor do they have any explanation for the old mines, many of them no longer lost, where Indian slaves labored their lives away. Yes, the Old Spanish Trail is real!

CHAPTER TEN

WAR IN THE MOUNTAINS

"For ye know that ye were not redeemed with corruptible things as silver and gold."

—Bible: 1 Peter 1:18

During the second half of the seventeenth century the slave trade flourished as never before. Jesuit Priests were charged with protecting the Indians, and in order to do so they were given the right to exploit their service as a slave for twenty years in exchange for civilizing them and saving their souls from purgatory. Priests taught the Indians the fear of damnation, and then used that fear to keep them at never ending hard labor. Once more thousands of Indians were dying in the mines, and once more an Indian leader was rising to save his people. He was called Pope, and he seemed to be everywhere, always urging the Indians to revolt. There is some evidence that Pope was aided by a mulatto named Diego de Naranjo who claimed to be a sorcerer and who had a certain following among the Indians at Taos. The Spanish made every effort to capture Pope, but with no success. Meanwhile countless Indians were dying from overwork and starvation, and many were on the verge of revolt, but the time wasn't ready, not quite.

In 1661 Governor Diego de Penalosa asked the king's permission to lead an expedition to locate a quicksilver mine Indians had told him was in Teguayo, not far from Sierra Azul, the legendary blue mountain of silver. The journeys and explorations of Don Diego Penalosa, Governor of New Mexico, have long been misunderstood and misrepresented. Various historians have called him a mere adventurer, or worse yet, an outright liar, but documents recorded by the Franciscan Father Nicholas de Freytas in 1663 but not discovered until 1856 in the Spanish archives at Seville reveal not only the importance of his discoveries, but more importantly the mines located in the northern mountains which he learned of but was not allowed to investigate.

Diego Penalosa was born at Lima, Peru in 1624 where after the best possible education and through influential family connections he rose through the ranks of alcalde to become a justice. Later he was appointed Captain of Infantry and in time was promoted to Governor of the Province of Omasuyas. The Duke of Albuquerque influenced him to come to Mexico, where in 1661 he became Governor and Captain-General of all New Mexico. After arriving at Santa Fe he learned of a kingdom far to the north which Indians called Teguayo, said to be very rich in mines of silver and gold. In 1662 Penalosa set out on a journey to discover those lands, but failed to reach them by being forced to detour far to the northeast in order to investigate reports of French incursions into Spanish territory. Nevertheless, the did learn much about Teguayo, which Father Freytas recorded.

On March 6th, 1662, Penalosa led a force of eighty Spaniards with Michael de Noriega as their Captain and Father Freytas as their Chaplin, accompanied by one thousand Indian bearers and 36 wheeled carts to carry supplies as well as a large coach and a portable chair for his Lordship. To investigate reports of the French they turned to the northeast, for a time following the century old trail of Coronado. They reached the Missouri River and turned up what is believed to be the Platte. Travelling further they encountered Indians "who gave his Lordship such grand accounts of the country ahead that it greatly excited our admiration."

Those Indians of the north told of mines located near the French lands of Aca-nada (Canada), "where the abundance of silver and gold is such that all vessels are made of silver, and in some cases of gold." They also gave Penalosa an account "of the great Lake of Copalla, where the richest mines of Moqtegsuma (Montezuma) are located, from which mines came the gold stones the Governor bought by barter." But Penalosa found himself separated from the riches of Teguayo "by a very lofty sierra, which the inhabitants of these regions do not know the termination of."

The explorers traced their trail back to Santa

Fe, intending to seek a shorter route to Teguayo, a route Father Freytas said the Indians told them must be "by way of Thoas (Taos), which is the most direct way, to towns which are seventy leagues hence in a straight line north to where those kingdoms begin." But on his return to Santa Fe Pensalosa had the misfortune to fall into the hands of the inquisitors of the Inquisition, and he was arrested on charges of "unrestrained language against the priests and blasphemy." He was taken to Mexico City in chains where he was imprisoned for 32 months. On his release he was fined all of his personal wealth and possessions and was banished to Spain, forbidden to ever return to the new world.

Governor Penalosa appealed his case to the Spanish Crown to no avail, and afterwards tried to sell his services to both the French and British governments, promising to lead them to lands far richer than any the Spanish had yet conquered, "A land that abounds in mines of gold, silver, copper, lead and other metals. In that land there is said to be a large lake of fresh water, one of excessive size, which drains into a lake of salt, where there is a mineral land of gold and of excellent brass. These lands can be discovered after the manner of the Spanish, deriving great advantage from them, besides paying duties to his Majesty." Penalosa never returned to the new world, but his pleadings to the French monarch eventually led to the expedition of La Salle and the French claim to the Mississippi Valley.

At nearly the same time, Governor Antonio de Otermin, who had succeeded Governor Penalosa, arranged a treaty with the Utes to stop their warfare against his settlers. The treaty was advantageous to the Utes because the Governor agreed to purchase slaves from them, primitive people like the Piedes and Shivwits, who the Utes traded for horses and trade goods. By 1700 the Utes had developed such a lucrative trade with the Spanish that they were selling or trading horses to the Shoshoni, Blackfoot and other tribes as far north as Wyoming and Montana. The treaty also allowed more miners to travel unmolested in the northern mountains. New mines were developed in places where prospectors had not dared go before, into the Uinta Mountains, the Boise Basin and the Wind River Range. The name Alonzo de Leon—

1669 inscribed on a cliff at Dry Fork Canyon near Vernal, Utah, reveals the early date miners were working there.

For a half dozen years there was a lull in the fighting between Spaniard and Ute, but in 1675 an incident occurred which fanned the flames of warfare once more and soon led to the greatest Indian revolt of all time. In that year, Pope, the Indian shaman who had been urging revolt, was captured by the Spaniards, but instead of being quickly killed, he was publicly whipped to disgrace him in the eyes of his followers. He was then jailed pending a public hanging, but with the help of allies he escaped and became a hero to his people. Secretly conferring with chiefs and medicine men throughout the mountains, plans were made that when a sign was given Indians all across the Great Basin country and from the Rio Grande to California would join in a great rebellion to overthrow the Spaniards.

In 1677 Friar Juan Francisco wrote a letter to the viceroy, asking him to stop the abuse of the Indians, and warning that a revolt was near. His plea fell on deaf ears, so in 1679 he journeyed to Mexico City where he presented the plight of the Indians to the Bishop. He was told that helping the Indians "was a useless and needless expense." Before Friar Francisco could return to his mountain mission a horrible accident occurred at the ancient Chalchihuitl Mine. As many as 100 Indians were killed at the bottom of the pit when a large section of the shaft side collapsed and buried them alive. It quickly ignited the spark of revolt.

It is almost impossible now to understand how in such primitive times, Pope, a simple Indian from the San Juan Pueblo, could coordinate such a successful revolt of Indians of many different nations and languages over such a wide region. If it were not so well documented in both church and civil records at such prestigious depositories as the Archivo General y Publico at Mexico City and the Spanish Archives of New Mexico at Santa Fe, it would be unbelievable. Pope himself believed, and he apparently convinced his followers, that he was in direct communication with the Emperor Montezuma and the God Quetzalcoatl, so that they could not fail in driving the Spanish from their land. The overthrow was extremely well coordinated and attacks were made simultaneously at every village, ranch, mine and mission.

As the first light of dawn came to Taos on August 10th, 1680, the overthrow and murder of hundreds, perhaps thousands, of miners, traders, merchants and clergy began. More than 400 Spaniards at the supply towns of Chama and Abique were quickly killed, while countless others at isolated mines and missions in the north were murdered or never heard from again. Everywhere the Spanish were taken by surprise and overwhelmed by sheer numbers, with very few escaping. The Jesuit Priests who were also mine owners had been among the most cruel to the Indians, and the Indians directed much of their vengeance against them. Not even Friar Francisco who had appealed their cause was spared. Many priests were killed at their own altars while praying for deliverance, as happened at Taos where Pope himself led the attack. Among them were Fray Francisco de Mora and Fray Antonio de Pro, as well as the town alcalde (mayor) and fifteen soldiers with all their families. More than 20 priests were killed at outlying missions and even more at the settlements. Priests were killed at San Idlefonso, Santa Clara, Thesuque, Nambe, San Marcos, Los Pecos, Cerrillos and Santo Domingo as well as at dozens of unnamed visitas in the mountains. Four padres who were living peacefully at the "Moqui Villages" died in the first assault.

Very few priests escaped, and none had time to take their church treasures with them. Almost every church document and record was lost, or were hidden so that few have ever been found. Gold and silver chalices, crosses and statues of the Virgin and the Saviour were hastily buried or thrown into wells or down mine shafts. Millions of

Bars of gold and silver bullion were buried or hidden at every mine and mission in the mountains. *(Courtesy Utah State Historical Society.)*

pieces of gold and silver collected as tithe were hidden under altars, concealed in places their owners hoped to return to or hidden in a hundred secret places. Records of bullion paid as the Royal Fifth were scrupulously kept, and they reveal that $10,000,000 had been collected from mines in the north, much of it from El Mina del Tiro. The great hoard of heavy metal bars which had accumulated could not be taken in the hasty exodus, as a reported $14,000,000 in tithes and church treasure was hidden in a mine shaft somewhere north of Taos. When the Spaniards returned nearly two decades later the mine had been so cleverly concealed that the treasure was never found.

That priests actually hid their church treasures is proven in the writings of Father Francisco Kino under similar circumstances. Although in California instead of New Mexico, the Indians at his mission also rose in revolt and killed priests, stole livestock and burned buildings. We know that there were mines near his mission, for Father Kino wrote: "In these new lands there are many good mineral veins of silver and gold, and even in sight of this mission some very good gold." Records from Father Kino's mission tell the story of the revolt there.

"During the revolt they killed Father Saeta, and throughout the valley they killed dozens more. While Father Kino waited the onslaught, Father Campos was also killed and all the others fled, leaving him alone. Lieutenant Manje alone returned and helped Father Kino hide the church treasure in a nearby cave. When Lieutenant Manje fled also, Father Kino alone remained and awaited his attackers. He survived and in time recovered the treasure and rebuilt his mission." Many such treasures were hidden at mines and missions across the Great Basin, but unlike Father Kino, few padres lived through the onslaught or returned to reclaim their treasures. But even today old maps and waybills are found, and for those who can decipher their cryptic meanings, church treasures can still be found.

Almost in a day every vestige of Spanish rule north of approximately the present Mexican border was obliterated. Almost none of the miners or others escaped, although a very few did make their way back to the border settlements over the next few years. Great numbers of Indian slaves were freed and large numbers of Spanish horses and weapons were seized by them. At mines throughout the far north, bars of gold and silver bullion were left stacked in mine tunnels or hastily buried near arrastra sites. In a few instances those who managed to escape later made maps or wrote waybills to lead others to their caches, but few have been found, for few waybills were comprehensible to the finder.

Miners, traders and priests were all driven back to Santa Fe, but even there they were not safe. Governor Oterman was wounded severely, as were many others. His later report stated: "I lost much blood from two arrow wounds I had received in the face, and from a remarkable gunshot wound on the chest." At Santa Fe some 2,500 Indians attacked the city and cut off the irrigation ditchs which supplied water to the settlers there. They then set fire to all the buildings. In his report the Governor stated, "The Indian leader approached, carrying two flags, one of white and one of red. If we chose the one of white, we must agree to leave the country immediately, but if we chose the one of red we must perish, for the rebels were many and we were very few." There was no alternative, so to avoid death from fire and thirst, Governor Otermin led a forced evacuation southward in which hundreds of Indians and dozens of Spaniards were killed. By sheer weight of numbers, the Indians overwhelmed their oppressors. Old records reveal that not counting the casualties at Santa Fe and the nearby settlements, at least another 379 colonists were killed in addition to 21 priests, while the number of soldiers murdered is unknown. No one knows how many miners and traders were killed in the distant mountains.

The rout was complete, with the Spanish being driven south beyond El Paso del Norte, and across the Rio Grande into Mexico. In Arizona the Indians reclaimed their land south to the Planchas del Plata Mine south of Tucson, while not even distant California was spared, the few Spanish explorers and missionaries there being driven south to Baja. It would be twelve long years before the reconquest of the north was begun, and long after that until it was completed. All of the northern borderlands were reclaimed by the Ute, Navajo and Commanche. After the revolution was complete, the Indians took great care to remove or destroy everything Spanish, so that should their oppressors ever return they would find nothing. Mine shafts were filled in, or if very deep covered with logs and soil. Tunnels were walled over or slide rock from the mountainside loosened to cover them. Stone or adobe missions were knocked down and their remains scattered to remove every sign of them. Log or brush cabins and visitas were burned. Everything Spanish was destroyed or concealed. It took a long time and much work, but the Indians had a lot of time and they were used to hard work.

Indians found many of the church and mine treasures left by the Spaniards. Without exception they were buried even deeper or moved to some other place and hidden again. Long afterwards descendants of the Indians sometimes told tales of buried treasure, and in some cases old maps or waybills were found in secret hiding places where the mines or missions had been. It was during that time that many legends of lost or buried treasure were born. And most of them are true, for they are based on true accounts.

CHAPTER ELEVEN

RECONQUERING THE NORTH

"For where your treasure is, there will your heart be also."

—Bible, Matthew 6:19

Even though the Spanish had been driven from the north at high cost in both lives and property, their interest in the gold and silver there or in saving Indian souls never waned, so they began to mke plans for their return. No doubt many small parties slipped quietly back into the mountains even before the reconquest began. As early as March, 1685, Pedro de Abalos appeared before the governor to file claim to a mine he had worked before the revolt. It was known as El Mina Nuestra Senora de Pilorde Sarogossa and was located in the Sierra Fray Cristobal, now the San Andreas Mountains of New Mexico.

In 1686 the elderly Father Alonzo de Posada, the same who had reported the capture of Indian slaves near the Great Salt Lake in 1630, outfitted an expedition to return to Teguayo, "To explore even the lands which are beyond the Yutahs." After the Spanish were driven from the mountains, French trappers and traders lost no time moving into those northern provinces. In 1689 Baron La Houton, Lord-Lieutenant of New France, travelled up the "long river," a major branch of the Mississippi, no doubt the Missouri, on a journey which took him six weeks. Four slaves he had with him guided his party west "into the land of the Guacsitares" and told him of another Indian nation beyond which they called the "Guasvatas," who lived "where a great river flowed into a salt lake, 300 leagues in circumference and 30 leagues wide, which is navigable by boats." So rapidly were white men returning to the mountains that in 1690 the Utes formed an alliance with their old enemies, the Navajos, to keep the Spanish away, but they underestimated both the strength and cunning of the Spaniards.

In Spain, Charles II had no intention of losing New Spain to France or anyone else. He ordered an army assembled to reconquer the north and sent Diego Jose de Vargas as its Captain-General. Vargas arrived at El Paso del Norte in February,

1691, where he found the king's army so badly decimated that it took nearly two years to ready the troops for an assault on the north. There is no doubt of the goal set by the king, and it was gold, not souls, as is recorded in the journals of Captain-General Vargas. He did not have sufficient men to train as soldiers, so he plead with the Viceroy, "Send convicts and mechanics from the jails, to serve as soldiers and to search for metals." In a letter written to the Count of Galve he wrote, "I shall take the risk at any cost to find the mines, and dispose of the apprehension about their stories, all of which appears so wonderful!"

On August 21st, 1692, Vargas started north with a well trained army, accompanied by some two dozen Franciscan Friars. Apparently he did not think it wise to venture into Indian territory with the hated Jesuits. He found deserted posts and camps all along the way, where every building had been burned or destroyed. He was aware that he was being watched by Indians at every step, but his army was too strong to be attacked. Vargas arrived at Santa Fe on September 12th, where he found the Governor's palace, or courthouse, in ruin but still the only building still intact. Mission San Miguel, built in 1610 had also been burned, but its stone walls remained. It was later rebuilt and today, nearly 375 years later, it still serves as the oldest church in the nation. An Indian appeared at the courthouse and told Vargas that if he would send his army and cannon away, they would talk. Against all advice he left his army at the edge of the foothills and walked to the courthouse alone. He embraced the chief who came from the building, at which signal two Franciscan Priests came forward and met the Indians, where a peace treaty was made. Vargas called it "his happy conquest."

As far north as Santa Fe the reconquest had been easy, for Indians were few while the army was large. The Northern Utes, Navajos and Comman-ches had not been encountered yet, but when

Like other adventurers before him, Vargas left his name at Morro Rock, sign post of the desert.

Vargas attempted to venture further north he met strong resistance. Taking 100 soldiers with 18 Priests and a herd of 900 cattle, 1,000 mules and 2,000 horses, Vargas pushed north from Santa Fe. Indian opposition was strong, with his little army being attacked from every quarter. Even the weather turned against him, for it became so cold that 21 of his party froze to death. In short order the Indians stampeded most of his livestock and drove Vargas and his men back to Santa Fe. With his army reunited, Vargas resorted to warfare, and with cavalry and cannon he captured hundreds of Indians. He ordered 70 of them hung in the public square, which stopped much of the resistance. Still, it took him two years more just to reclaim Taos, Chama and Abique.

Late in 1694 Vargas reestablished a mission in the San Luis Valley of Colorado, from which mining parties began returning to the mountains. Captain Rogue de Madrid returned to his father's mine, which he was able to find only with the use of a waybill and map. He discovered that Indians had filled the shaft with stones and soil so that it appeared impossible to reopen it. Many of the mines which had been worked before the revolt could not be found again, so cleverly had the Indians concealed them. It has been suggested that some mines were concealed not only to hide their locations, but for religious purposes as well. In several places shafts were filled with soil or rock different from that found anywhere nearby. In several instances the Indians had gone to great labor to carry from long distances sufficient material to fill a shaft one hundred feet or more in depth. A padre asked why this had been done, when in some cases no effort had been made to erase the scar left on the mountainside by the mine, or to hide arrastras which were in plain sight. The Indian's answer was that the gold belonged to the Sun God, and must not be possessed by anyone whose God was not the Sun God.

Shafts were filled with rock or covered with tree trunks, often with grass, sage or other brush planted atop them. Only those having an accurate map or well written waybill were able to return to the mines after twenty years or more. But some new mines were also discovered, as was described by Fray Agustin de Vetancurt in his Cronica de la Provinciadel Santo Evangelico. "There we found a bald and rocky mountain where there are found ores, or veins of lead and silver. There is also a vein of lodestone, and another where there is gypsum as transparent as glass."

In 1692 Captain-General Diego de Vargas was seized and placed under arrest by the Bishop of New Mexico for his cruelties to the Indians, and also because he had displayed greater interest in riches than he had in saving souls. Governor Rodriguez Cabero kept Vargas incarcerated in a tiny cell for three years. In time he was pardoned, but was not allowed to return to his army in the north. He was reinstated to his rank of Captain-General by order of the king in 1703, but he died from the effects of his long imprisonment and ill treatment only a few months later, in April, 1704. The life of a conquistadore was never an easy one. As a tribute to his service to the king, twelve head of cattle were killed and their meat along with fifty measures of wheat were given to the poor Indians at Santa Fe. It was little enough, considering the risks and pain he had suffered.

By the early 1700s most of the regions once explored by Spain had been reclaimed from the Indians; however, many of the mines which had been worked by the Spaniards twenty to thirty years before could not be located by their owner's sons or others sent to find them. Most of those who had worked at them had been killed in the revolt of 1680 or had since died, while the memory of others was no longer clear enough to find their way back into the mountains. One particularly rich and well known mine where shafts had been filled in and every trace of its workings concealed was found through the use of a waybill which had been passed down through family members, El Mina Nuestra Senora de los Reyes de Linares, in what was then called the San Luzaro Mountains.

In 1705 Roque de Madrid led a punitive expedition north from Taos to capture and return runaway slaves, evidence that once more Indians were being forced to work in mines and at ranches. Madrid's route is uncertain, but he travelled beyond the four corners area of Utah and Colorado, to "Sierra del Cobre and Arroyo del Belduque." That same year, 1705, the fabled land of Teguayo was first shown on the famous maps of Englishman John Harris. Although Teguayo was spelled Thongo, the maps still showed the great Lake of Copalla being drained by the mythical San Bueneventura River, which flowed across the Nevada deserts into San Francisco Bay. His map

was frequently used by French and British trappers and perhaps by a few adventuresome Spaniards as well.

The year following, Juan de Uribarri pursued runaway slaves north into the San Pete Valley of central Utah. Uribarri led a second expedition in 1709 to the furtherest limits of Spanish control, where he met French fur traders who had travelled west from the Mississippi. He took possession of "the northern frontier, north of the Rockies," in the name of the king. While pursuing the runaways he discovered one of the mines worked before 1680 and upon his return to Santa Fe declared a mining claim to it before Governor Villasenor. During the same time that Uribarri was at the northern limits of New Mexico, a mine was discovered and worked on the St. Mary's River of northern Idaho. Whether it was found by Uribarri or someone else

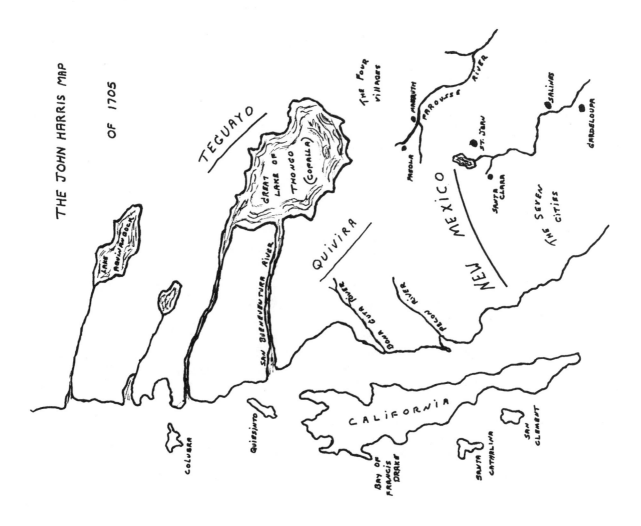

is unknown, but in 1882 a map showing the mine and Lake Coeur d' Alene was found in the Spanish archives of New Mexico at Santa Fe. On its edge was written in archaic Spanish, "Follow the west shore of the lake to where a large river enters it, and follow upstream to its first fork, which is to be followed to the second branch from the east. Ascend that creek for one league, from which place the mine lies 1,000 varas to the south." A search was made the following year, but the old mine was not found, nor has anyone found it since, although someone may, some day.

If the finding of a Spanish mine as far north as the panhandle of Idaho seems to be in conflict with some teachings, consider the following: In 1981 a Spanish sword and a small bronze cannon were found on Vancouver Island. A year later a prospector who decided to investigate the area more closely discovered a place where steps had been cut into a stone cliff, and following them he came upon an unknown cavern in which he located a copper chest containing some ancient tools, the decayed remains of a leather bound journal written in Spanish and two gold bars, 1"x1½"x3" in size, each marked "Oro—1709"!

As more old mines were relocated and new ones discovered, the need for Indian labor increased, and once more slaving became a lucrative business. The Utes were rapidly becoming a wealthy people from selling slaves to the Spaniards, who they captured as far north as Wyoming and Montana. In an attempt to curb the power of the Utes and hopefully to subjugate them, the Viceroy instituted a new policy which he called "Reduccion." He planned to bribe the Utes with gifts and liquor and undermine their social structure, so they would gradually be assimilated into a half-breed or mestizo society, and thus cease to exist. But his plan never worked, for apparently there were too many Utes and too few Spaniards.

The slave trade so prospered that Indian children were being sold as household servants as far south as Chihuahua. Many illegal slaving parties began to venture into the desert areas north of Utah Valley and west into Nevada. In 1712 Governor Ignacio Mogollon found it necessary to forbid all unlicensed traders from going into Ute country. But there were so many ways slavers could enter the mountains that his orders could not be enforced, all that could be done was to arrest and fine those caught selling slaves. There are many references in the Spanish Archives which reveal that by 1720 many Spaniards were trading in slaves in the area of Utah Valley. So great were the profits made through slavery that French Jesuits began entering the region from the northwest. They came from as far away as the Great Lakes region where they had already located mines of copper and lodestone. Their trails began to overlap the older trails of their brother priests made long before.

French Governor Bienville of Louisiana made a treaty with the Commanches allowing him to build Fort Cavaynolle on the Missouri River, from which trade trails were blazed into the western mountains to compete with Spanish traders already there. Some of his first trading parties were under the guidance of Fabry Bruyere. So great became the threat of French and British traders that in 1719 Pedro de Villasur and Father Minguez with 45 soldiers and 60 Indian servants were sent to stop their incursions into Spanish territory. Villasur travelled north into Colorado where he turned northwest into the Uinta Mountains of Utah, continued into Wyoming and then journeyed eastward to Nebraska. Of interest is the fact that in 1961 a Spanish sword of the type used in Villasur's time was found near Dayton, Wyoming, in a remarkable state of preservation. It is now on display at a museum there.

Villasur's instructions were to establish missions in the north from which the country might be populated, rancherias built and the mines protected. Somewhere along the way, perhaps where one of his missions was built, the party came into possession of a large treasure of silver bullion. Some believe it was recovered from one of the old mines of the Uintas where it was cached during the revolt of 1680. On August 13th, 1720, Villasur's party was attacked by a large force of Indians, said to be led by a French Jesuit Priest. Nearly all of his men were annihilated, only 13 surviving to make their way back to the settlements on the San Juan. They reported that they buried their great treasure along a stream where they had been building a mission. There is no record that either the mission or its hidden treasure has ever been found; however, a clue might be found in recent research.

Doctor Moormon of Utah's Weber State

College has spent a great deal of time investigating the line of missions established by Villasur. He is convinced that one of those missions was built soon after 1700 north of Duchesne, Utah, probably on Rock Creek. If it was not actually built by Villasur, it was an earlier mission used and improved on by him. There is a great deal of reason to believe Dr. Moormon is correct, from Indian traditions which tell of a mission in that area, to references found in church archives and old names, dates and church symbols found close by. Physical evidence such as Spanish type spurs, bronze church bells and Catholic crosses have been found along Rock Creek, as have cannons and cannon balls dating from the seventeenth century. The rubble stone ruins of an ancient structure believed to have been the mission itself, with the graves of Europeans nearby have also been found.

Dr. Moormon located descriptions of a mission which was located at a "real of mines" which fits almost exactly the mines in the Rock Creek area. Marriage and baptismal records kept by a mission clerk were studied in the library of a mission in Mexico. There have been too many finds of Spanish artifacts in the Rock Creek area over greatly separated periods of time by people totally unaware of each other to ignore. The number of ranchers, hunters, fishermen and prospectors who have seen old cannons, or found parts and pieces of them, are too numerous to list. There is no doubt they were placed there to guard the old mission. That there is also a Catholic cemetery is also certain, for equally as many have seen it. Several years ago one of the graves was dug into by

Who can solve the mystery of Rock Creek's forgotten mission and its lost treasure?

someone using a metal detector. Several skeletons still having remnants of old fashioned European style clothing clinging to the bones were found, as well as several pieces of gold which had attracted the metal detector.

Not long before, in 1953, well known author C. Kutac, while exploring the area described the cannons, ancient Spanish signs, the ruins of an arrastra and his discovery of a Catholic cross of the type worn by padres during the seventeenth century. In 1963 Gale Rhoades, while investigating the same area, made the discovery of several old graves where he found an old bronze bell of ancient design. It is almost identical to a similar bell found at a mission ruin near Blanding, Utah, in 1971, which bell was later judged to be more than 500 years old. The Rock Creek area is also the center of an old Spanish mining area, where such famed mines as the Mine of Lost Souls were once worked. And if the research completed by those interested in the mission and nearby mines is correct, Rock Creek Canyon may also be the site of one of the richest mines ever, the famous Lost Rhoades, as well as one of the greatest treasures ever hidden, the fabulous Jaredite Treasure!

In time nearly every area where there had been an old Spanish mine or mission had its tale of Jesuit treasure. Many were only oral legends, but nevertheless quite authentic because they were first hand accounts told by Indians who remembered the old Spanish places. One Ute legend was told to the first pioneers to settle in Utah's Uinta Basin. "Many years ago, even before my father was born, the Black Robes who lived at the old mission in the land of the Utes had mines of silver and gold where they made my people work very hard. Why they wanted to much metal no one knew, for they couldn't eat it, but still they collected every piece they could find and hid it away in some secret place at their little church. Some said it was being hoarded to send to their chief who lived across the big water.

"But there came a time when the Black Robes received a very troublesome message, and very quickly they had our people help them conceal every sign of their mines and the place where they hid their treasure. The very next day they were seized by their own people who had arrived in the night, and they were taken away in chains, the very same chains they had placed on our fathers. No one knew where they were taken or if they would ever return. After they left, our people removed every trace of their mission and our chief medicine man placed a curse on their mine, that whoever should return to it, his blood would turn to water and he would die a thousand deaths. Even today none of our people will go near that place!"

In 1969 a most amazing treasure tale was told to the author by a man who not only found the old mission site, but actually saw its treasure. The site was located from a waybill "obtained at great cost," which placed the mission at the center of a "real of mines." Birth, death and baptismal records he examined indicated there was a major Indian school there also, and that the mission was built before the revolt of 1680. The records contained an order directed by the king himself, which stated, "I also order and command that at the mines, a church shall be built, so that all of the Indians who labor at the mines may hear Mass on the said days, and I also command that the miners who bring the Indians to mine gold must observe with them the same procedures which are followed elsewhere, under the same penalties and in the same manner." The waybill itself was very long and rambling, and because it was written in both Latin and Spanish, it was very difficult to translate, but in effect it was as follows:

"From the monastery and church buildings, all of which were built for the glory of God, cross the river to a round shaped hill, which is flat on top and covered with grass. At the base of this hill, which faces the setting sun, you will find an opening and at its end a great chamber, which took many workers more than two years to hollow out. At the portal you must take great care in opening the door, which is a very heavy one. You must examine it very closely, for the dead do not talk! When you have unlatched the door, you will find an image of pure gold one vara in height, the eyes of which are two large emeralds. The image was placed there for the good of mankind. Exercise great care in passing through the tunnel, for a trap is there for those not ordained to enter. The chamber itself is lighted and well made, and is strengthened by blocks of stone three estados or more in height. Great care must be taken on entering this room, for enough poison has been laid about to trouble the unsuspecting. In the center of the chamber is a great pile of cast bars of such great weight that it took much labor to place them there. When the bars are moved a flat stone will be revealed, under which is another chamber where there are 140 heaps of gold, and a box containing 130,000 pieces of gold and silver. This great treasure represents 15 years of work in the mines by more than 500 nephites, all directed by the King's most reverent and faithful servants of God."

Both the discoverer and a partner had been evicted from the Ute lands with strong warnings not to return; nevertheless, they did return and actually saw and handled the treasure. But they were seen by Indians who shot his partner and narrowly missed hitting him. For that reason as well as certain religious beliefs, the finder must remain anonymous, and some details about him withheld; however, the details of his amazing find are essentially as follows: After locating the general area of the mission from the waybill, its exact site was found by the use of an instrument similar to a dowsing rod. Since it is not in a mineralized area, the instrument was attracted by the cache described in the waybill. Entering the reservation lands on foot from the mountains, they came to the mission site. Foundation stones and a few low rock walls could be seen in the brush, as well as a place where cedar posts protruded a few inches above ground level, where watch towers had been built. Three Spanish cannons with bores of approximately three inches were discovered on a rock ledge above the mission site. They were green with vertigris and appeared to be made of bronze. Two burial places were found also, one for Spanish miners and one for Indians.

Crossing the river (Rock Creek) from the mission as directed in the waybill, they noticed an opening about two feet in diameter. It could not be seen except by someone wading in the river, and was nearly overgrown with tree roots. Investigating, they discovered that a tunnel went straight into the hillside from the river. The finder crawled into the hole where he discovered that within a few feet it opened into a tunnel large enough to stand in. A large brass spike driven into the wall had apparently been used to hang a torch of some kind on. There was also a niche in the wall where the golden idol may have stood, but it appeared that the river during past flood stages had washed much of the portal away, probably including the heavy door and causing the idol to fall into the river.

In a short distance the tunnel floor dropped into "a water trap of ingenious design," but taking a flashlight wrapped in plastic he took a deep breath and felt his way for some thirty or forty feet under water to where the floor rose above water level. Beyond, the tunnel led to a large room cut from solid rock. In each corner of the room there was a cedar post with its top hollowed out, each post having "a pine pitch candle" which had provided light for the room. In the center of the cavern there was a large square pile of stacked gold and silver bars. Each bar was approximately 4"x6" in size and about 20" long. There were 80 bars. He counted them, and counted them again. But the bars were so heavy he couldn't lift them. After he went back through the "water trap" his partner entered the chamber, and he too counted 80 bars. At the price of gold and silver in 1969 they estimated their value at $600,000,000!

Since it was nearly nightfall they made camp across the river, intending to return to the treasure in the morning; however, at dawn's first light two Indian game wardens, who apparently thought they were fishermen, came into their camp and ordered them off reservation land. Every time they tried to return, something happened to prevent

Heavy bars of silver and gold are still cached at the Jaradite treasure cave.

them from getting close to the old mission site. It was during one of those later trips that his partner was shot. Finally convinced that the Indians did not know of the cache, he attended a tribal meeting where he asked for a permit to prospect on reservation land. From the questions asked by the tribal council, he learned that the Indians were aware of the mission site and considered it a sacred place because of the graves there. Many questions were asked about what he intended to search for, and when he refused to divulge any further details, a permit was refused.

The finder is convinced the Indians do not know of the cache, or if they do, are afraid to go near it. He must remain anonymous for the reasons already cited, but he says he will never return to the old mission on Rock Creek. Financially well fixed, he does not need the treasure, but more important, he values his life more than the gold!

CHAPTER TWELVE

EXPLORATIONS OF RECORD

"There is gold, and a multitude of rubies."

—Bible, Book of Proverbs

For more than 200 years Spanish pack trains heavily laden with gold and silver carried hundreds of millions of dollars in treasure from the mines of the Americas to seaports like Carthagena, Veracruz, Padre Island and Galveston. The huge wealth came from the Inca and Aztec empires of New Spain and the Indian nations of New Mexico. The treasures were loaded aboard flotillas of galleons called plate fleets, to be carried to the Royal Vaults at Seville in Spain. The immensity of the treasure sent to the Spanish kings staggers the imagination, but records at the Archivo General de Indios de Seville and at the Biblioteca de Madrid verify their almost unbelievable worth.

From 1495 to 1555 the treasure's value totaled 100 million dollars, most of it in gold. After 1555 most of the total was in silver, as mining activity moved from Mexico to regions now in the western United States. The total from 1555 to 1700 was 2½ billion dollars, and from 1700 to 1820, when the last plate fleet sailed, five billion dollars more was shipped. In addition, most historians believe that another ten billion dollars in personal wealth, contraband and unregistered treasure was also shipped to Spain. As much as 20 billion dollars altogether, more than the mind can comprehend!

But as already described, a huge amount of treasure never reached its destination. A list of the Spanish treasure galleons lost to pirates and hurricanes would fill a large volume, but even a partial list reveals not only the treasure lost, but also gives some idea of the large amount of gold and silver the Spanish mines actually produced. Included in the list of lost treasure galleons is the Trinidad in 1540 with $4 million, the Capitana in 1563 with $3 million, the Los Chagos in 1594 with $5 million, the Ambrosio in 1605 with $3 million, the Senor de Atocha in 1622 with $4 million and the Almiranta in 1656 with $3 million aboard. Listed are only a few of the treasure ships lost, and those only to the revolt of 1680. Hundreds of

millions more were lost after 1700. In retrospect, one can't help but wonder why the voyages of the plate fleets weren't better planned, to sail by other routes to avoid pirates or earlier in the year to miss the hurricane season.

An interesting account of how one ship load of silver was saved from the pirates was written by Father Kino in 1710. "We left about 400 souls in the interior and went to the harbor of Matonchal at New Galacia. There Viceroy Don Thomas Marfus sent us to meet and warn a treasure ship, since at that time the Pickilinques Pirates were visiting that region for ships to rob. Meeting the ship within ten days, thanks be to God, and putting to sea with her so that she should neither come to land or be seen by her enemies, we all arrived safely at Acapulco, having rescued four or five millions for the Royal Crown, and for his vassals without loss, in reward of the Very Catholic expenditures which the Royal Monarchy makes in honor of His Divine Majesty, and for the good of countless souls."

Nearly everyone is familiar with the millions in treasure which treasure hunter Mel Fisher has recovered from plate fleet wrecks off the coast of Florida. After 15 years of search he located the wreck of the treasure galleon Senor de Atocha on July 20th, 1985, at a depth of only 54 feet. In only four days his divers recovered $1,000,000 in gold and jewelry, including 13 gold bars, a gold chain more than six feet in length and gold bracelets encrusted with emeralds! But probably the most fantastic find was a huge mound of silver bars, piled on the bottom like great loafs of bread, weighing 75 pounds each. 800 bars weighing 30 tons were recovered in only several days, but so many remain that it is estimated that it will take 2½ years to recover all of them! Eight chests of minted coins were also found, including some 500,000 of silver valued at $1,000 each and thousands of doubloons of gold worth at least $5,000 each to collectors! Tons of silver bars are being recovered daily, along with priceless gold cups, chalices, candleabras and precious jewels. The find is estimated to be worth $400,000,000 at present prices, but the wealth of the Atocha is only a small part of the gold and silver that came from hundreds of now lost mines along the Old Spanish Trail.

Other treasure salvors like Kip Wagner and Bob Marx have also recovered millions in Spanish gold along the gulf coast, and during the past year, 1985, treasure hunter Barry Clifford located the lost ship Whidah, which went to the bottom off Cape Cod in 1717, carrying the loot from a dozen or more Spanish treasure galleons which its Captain Black Bellamy had pirated. Already Clifford has recovered a chest of Spanish coins minted before 1715, bars of gold and chests of jewels, as well as broadswords, flintlock pistols and more than 20 cannons. It is believed he will salvage more than $400,000,000! But the greatest plate fleet loss was yet to occur, leaving for today's salvors the largest lost treasure of all time.

From 1701 to 1713 Spain was engaged in the War Of Succession, during which time the king was afraid to ship any of his plunder from the new world, for fear it would fall into the hands of the British. Meanwhile pack trains continued to bring loads of heavy bullion to ports along the gulf coast, where it was piled waiting shipment to Spain. Baron Von Humboldt gave some idea of its great volume when he wrote, "Thousands of mules arrived every week carrying bars of silver and other treasure." When the war ended a fleet of galleons was dispatched to take the hoard of accumulated wealth to Seville. The ships were loaded with gold and silver at now forgotten ports and then dropped anchor together at Havana harbor, where the entire plate fleet was placed under the command of Admiral Don Juan Esteban de Ubilla.

Eleven treasure galleons left Havana on July 27th, 1715, far too late in the year, for it was already then the hurricane season. Its cargo included 14 million pesos in silver, tons of newly minted pieces of eight from the mint at Mexico City, holds so heavily loaded with bars of gold and silver bullion that the ships rode dangerously low in the water, and church treasure whose value was not listed, but which was said to be "beyond estimate." There was also personal wealth as well as contra-band and unregistered treasure equal to that listed on the ship's manifests.

On July 30th, ten of the eleven ships sank in a hurricane off the coast of Florida. More than 1,000 sailors were lost at sea, including Admiral Ubilla. Gold and silver coins from the 1715 plate fleet have been washing up onto Florida beaches for 250 years now, while treasure salvors at the wreck sites have salvaged tens of millions more in relics and artifacts. But most of the treasure lost in the wrecks of 1715, including the heavy bullion bars from the mines of New Mexico, are too heavy to ever be washed ashore, and so they still lie where they went down, covered with the sands of the ocean bottom, without doubt one of the world's greatest treasures.

The loss of the 1715 plate fleet probably went unknown to the miners and padres a thousand miles and more beyond the Spanish borderlands, at the lonely missions and isolated mines throughout the mountains of the west. Those mountains were rapidly becoming ever more crowded, for both legal and unauthorized parties pressed ever further northward. In 1740 Fray Carlos Jose Delgado led an expedition north to Teguayo, of which he later wrote: "There lives a king of such dignity and wealth that he neither speaks or looks at anyone, such is his serenity. His mines are the richest in all New Mexico. He lives in a land where there is a city so large that one cannot walk around it in eight days!"

Fray Delgado complained of the harsh treatment Indians received from alcaldes and other civil servants. He wrote that each year the Navajos were made to weave 400 blankets, which were taken from them without payment. Piutes who grew maize had it seized by the corregidores (magistrates), "Leaving these poor creatures with nothing to eat, and give them nothing in return but a few handfuls of tobacco. They have to submit to this great injustice or suffer severe punishment. These punishments are so cruel and inhuman that sometimes they are confined to the stocks, and I cannot say it without tears, but they flog them so pitilessly, they inflict such deep scars upon them that they remain for many years. When I went among the heathen, there were some among them who showed me their scars, and gave me to understand this was their reason why they had fled and did not return to the church."

In 1749 the Utes under Chief Don thomas made an alliance with the Spanish to wage war against the Commanches. The Spaniards were anxious to have a period of peace with the Utes, however brief, for they were not content to wait for the Utes to come to them to trade, but instead established outposts and visitas all across the Great Basin. For a time they traded freely from the San Juan to the Uinta Basin and from the Rockies to the deserts of western Nevada. But while the Spanish enjoyed a brief time of peace in the north, their Indian problems became worse in the south. In 1750 the Apaches joined forces with the usually peaceful Pimas to kill more than 100 people, including four priests. During his administration, Father Kino had been especially kind to the Indians at Tusayan, along the Gila River and south of the Colorado, but after his death newly assigned priests treated the Pimas as slaves, which resulted in the Pima Revolt, aided by the Apaches. Mines, settlements and missions were destroyed, from the Moqui villages to the mines at Potosi in southern Nevada. It took five long years before Spanish soldiers were able to force their way back into Pima country.

Meanwhile nearly every ore vein and placer in the northern mountains and deserts were being investigated by Spanish miners. At the edge of the desert in west-central Utah one of the richest silver deposits was being mined a few miles north of present day Minersivlle. In the foothills of a dry desert range, now the Mineral Mountains, Spanish miners sank an inclined shaft into a silver ledge. When it was rediscovered by Mormon settlers more than a century later, it would become known as the famous Lincoln Mine. Bars of silver-lead bullion were poured at a crude smelter there and then carried hundreds of miles by cargas (pack trains) across the deserts and canyonlands to the gulf coast.

Somewhere in the Henry Mountains under the shadow of 11,000' Mt. Ellen, Spaniards forced their Indian slaves to work endless hours in the famed El Mina Josephine de Martinique, according to their own records the richest mine of all. The methods used at the Josephine were crude, and depended upon an endless supply of free labor. Fires were built against the ore veins at the end of each tunnel or shaft bottom. After the rock was heated, water was thrown against it to crack and break the hard rock. It was a slow, tedious process, and ventilation was poor in the smoke and steam choked tunnels.

The broken rock was loaded into tenates, baskets made from cactus fiber or from leather, having a tump line or strap across the bearer's forehead. The loads carried weighed as much as 100 pounds. With the tenate carried high on his back and the tump line across his forehead taking much of the weight, the Indian slave would lean forward for balance as he shuffled along the dark tunnels or climbed precariously up chicken ladders braced into the steep sides of the shaft. The notched logs were much easier for the bare footed Indian to climb than were conventional ladders, and they left his hands free for balance or to carry a smouldering torch for light.

Young Indian boys were used to crawl back into small drifts or coyote holes, where they would gather the pieces of broken quartz in baskets and then drag them outside. There both older boys and girls would break the quartz boulders with heavy stones, crushing it to the size of beans. Experienced miners would watch closely and direct the separation of waste rock from good ore, generally saving only whatever appeared to be shiny or metallic. A lot of good ore with gold not visible to the eye was thrown onto waste dumps. The bean size pieces of ore were then dumped into an arrastra, where Indians, often two or three tied together side by side, turned the mill and dragged the heavy mill stone, which crushed the ore to the fineness of flour. 200 years later E.T. Wolverton found several of those ancient arrastras, and also many places where pieces of rich gold ore had been thrown away.

Even though mines like the Josephine have not been found in recent times, many clues to their locations have been. Holes worn into solid rock where an arrastra's center support pole stood and the well worn circular outline where the mill stone was dragged are still often found, usually near a small spring or water seep. Usually no trace of the mine itself can be found, but certainly they are not far from the arrastra sites. Sometimes quicksilver amalgam which escaped from the mill and into rock crevices can be recovered and retorted (evaporated over a fire), and is often rich in gold. After the revolt of 1680, most of the old Spanish mines were so well concealed that many like the Josephine have never been found. But others, like the Lincoln Mine, have been located and worked extensively for long periods of time at great profit.

An intriguing lost mine tale which had its origin in the 1756 expedition of Don Bernardo de Miranda, who with a small band of illegal miners set out to discover mines he had been told of. He located a natural cave which had veins of rich silver ore in it. The mine was worked for a short time, but when Miranda attempted to sell the silver from it, he was arrested by the king's tax collectors. He refused to tell where the treasure cave was located, although he said, "The cave is so rich that I will guarantee to give to every one who goes with me a full claim. The principal vein is more than two varas in width (five feet wide) and is of unknown length." Strangely, just such a cave was discovered not far from the already mentioned Lincoln Mine and was named the Cave Mine, where a small camp named Bradshaw City grew up seven miles north of Minersville. Miranda's story is very similar to that of Padre La Rue, sometimes called La Rux or La Cruz.

Padre La Rue oversaw a mission which depended upon cultivated fields for sustenance, but after a long drought ruined his mission fields, he guided his followers north to where Indian servants had told him a rich silver mine could be found. Such a mine, not authorized by the viceroy, was illegal, but nevertheless, the new mining camp prospered. Much silver was collected and smelted in vassos, adobe and stone furnaces, where it was poured into bullion bars. The people at Padre La Rue's settlement lived happily together, but when several years had passed and no report was received from him, soldiers were sent to investigate. Being warned of their approach, Padre La Rue had his great hoard of silver piled inside the cave's entrance and its opening concealed. All of his Indian servants were freed, and when the soldiers arrived where a new mission and fields were located, he refused to tell the mine's location, saying the silver belonged to God, not man. The good padre was tortured until he died, but his secret was not revealed.

Some treasure hunters believe that Padre La Rue's cache and the Doc Noss treasure on Victorio Peak are one and the same. On November 7th, 1937, Dr. Milton Noss was hunting deer on Victorio Peak in the San Andreas Mountains north of Las Cruces, New Mexico, in almost exactly the same area where Padre La Rue had his mine. Noss discovered a caving shaft high on the mountain and in a cavern at its bottom he found a treasure in gold bars and priceless artifacts beyond imagination. Over a period of several years Noss removed many of the heavy bars, as well as swords, silver bowls, candle holders and all sorts of church chalices, communion plates, baptismal fonts and other valuable objects. Many people saw and handled the items he recovered, so there is no question of their authenticity. Noss sold part of the treasure, but he cached even more. Many of the church artifacts are still owned by his wife and have been photographed and seen in many newspapers and national magazines recently, all as part of a legal dispute over their ownership. An assay made by a reputable firm proved the gold bars to be a bullion 63⅛ gold, 33⅛ copper and 3⅛ silver. They were judged to be 300 years old.

In 1939 while attempting to open the caved shaft so work could progress more quickly, Noss dynamited a protruding rock and caved the entire shaft. When he began to tunnel in the caved workings from lower on the mountin he became involved in lawsuits with the federal government, since the land in question is on the army's White Sands Testing Range. During an argument over some of the recovered treasure Noss was shot and killed. His widow hired attorney F. Lee Bailey, who was able to obtain a limited time permission from the army to excavate the treasure. Heavy equipment was brought in under the watchful eye of the IRS, and work began. The digging proved to be much more time consuming than first estimated, and when time ran out the army cancelled the lease. Since then the governor, several congressmen, dozen of attorneys and generals all the way to the Pentagon have become involved. Legal battles still continue, with Noss attorneys contending that the army has secretly removed the treasure, which they say exceeds five-hundred million dollars! The last chapter of the Doc Noss treasure hasn't been written, nor have we heard the last of Padre La Rue.

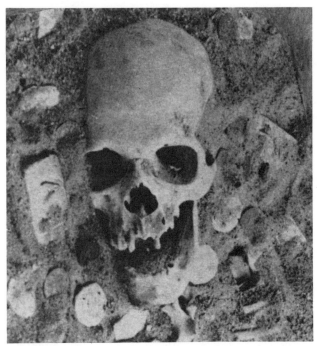

Ghosts of murdered miners still guard Doc Noss's lost mission treasure.

One of the earliest miners of Utah Valley who we find mentioned in historical records was Manuel Meastes, who packed bullion from the Mine of the Yutahs and others nearby in 1755. When in 1805 he was commended by Governor Alencaster for "more than fifty years service as an interpreter in the mountains of the north," Meastes said that mining and slaving were the most profitable things he had ever done. Shortly after Meastes began mining near Utah Valley in 1750, an only recently documented and somewhat controversial expedition was made through northern Colorado and far into Utah. In 1760 an Indian named Wolfskin brought a large silver ingot into the blacksmith shop of Jose Trujillo. The Indian told Trujillo that the ingot came a silver mine he knew of, and after trading it for a few trifles, he left town. Governor Tomas Cachupin was so intrigued by the valuable ingot and Wolfskin's tale that he ordered Father Juan Maria de Rivera to form a party of exploration to locate Wolfskin and his mine.

For many years prestigious historical societies of Colorado and Utah refused to accept the Rivera expedition as factual, as they do all early explorations regardless of the vast amount of physical evidence to the contrary, simply because no written proof or documentation prior to the Escalante expedition of 1776 can be found. Only recently Dr. Janet Fielman, representing Dr. Donald Cutler, Professor of History at the University of New Mexico uncovered the missing Rivera journals at the Servicio Historio Militar at Madrid, Spain, and proved that not only had Rivera preceded Escalante, he was actually following an even older trail, the Old Spanish Trail.

Father Rivera began his journey in search of Wolfskin in 1761, accompanied by Andres and Gregorio Sandoval, Antonio Martin, Andres and Lucrecio Muniz as guides and an Indian interpreter called Juachinielo, plus a number of genizaros. Fourteen soldiers also accompanied the expedition. Rivera travelled north through the La Plata (silver) Mountains, where he investigated the ancient Mt. Hesperas Mine, and then turned west, following the Dolores River into present Utah. Near Moab on the Colorado, Rivera carved "a large Catholic cross, the words Viva Jesus, and his own name and date on a large white poplar tree." Interestly, Father Escalante, according to some the first explorer into that area, himself reported finding the tree with Rivera's name on it! The "white poplar" tree was probably a cottonwood.

Although he searched even beyond the sierra de La Sal Mountains, Rivera failed to find Wolfskin. Discouraged, he made a long side trip to locate an old woman who Indians told him also knew where the silver mine was, but he failed to find her also. Research made by Dr. moorman, Weber State College in Ogden, Utah indicates tht the side trip made by Rivera was to the shores of Sevier Lke, near the Utah-Nevada border. Although Rivera failed to find either Wolfskin or the old Indian woman, he was told that if he returned with trade goods he might be shown the mine.

Rivera returned to the settlements along the San Juan where he outfitted another expedition. On his second trip into the mountains in 1765, Rivera took a great amount of trade goods, and he instructed all in his party not to give the Indians any reason to believe they were interested in mines, but only in trade. He took a different route on his second trip, following Dove Creek into Utah southeast of present Monticello, where he camped on October 6th, 1765. Rivera travelled north through Lisbon and Spanish valleys to the Sierra de La Sals, where he found Wolfskin. Rivera was told that in order to find the silver mines he should follow the edge of the mountains to the northwest, where he would come to a settlement where other white men lived by a stream in Mexican style houses. They wore heavy beards and dressed in buckskins, and spoke the same language as Rivera. Rivera later reported that he travelled for 150 leagues (nearly 400 miles) along the edge of the mountains, but never found the settlement. Note that such a journey would have taken him beyond the Uinta Mountains, likely into present day Idaho. Desperately in need of supplies, he returned to the San Juan settlements.

The search for the place where Wolfskin obtained his silver and the settlement there is of interest, for there were several such places at that time, among them the mission established by Villasur and the old Jesuit Mission on Rock Creek, which was by a stream where miners spoke the same language as Rivera. Of equal interest is an 1811 expedition made by Jose Rafael Sarracino in search of a lost Spanish settlement, which will be mentioned later. Another little known journey into the north was that of the Marquis de Rubi, Inspector of the Internal Provinces, on a tour of inspection with Maestro de Campo Nicloas de La Fora in 1766-67. His report reveals they journeyed beyond the La Plata Mountains "into the northern provinces, which are well known for one hundred leagues and more beyond New Mexico."

CHAPTER THIRTEEN
DEATH TO THE JESUITS

"Lay not up for yourselves treasures on earth,
Where moth and rust doth corrupt,
And where thieves break through and steal."

— Bible, Matthew 6:19

In June, 1767, the Viceroy and the highest ranking officials of all New Spain gathered at Mexico City to witness the unsealing of a secret order brought directly from King Carlos III. When opened, the sealed orders directed that under penalty of death and within 24 hours, every Jesuit Priest throughout all of New Spain and New Mexico was to be seized and returned to Spain in irons! The king's order, officially dated June 24th, 1767, was carried by his most trusted agent to the Viceroy himself. It read: "I hereby invest you with my complete and royal powers that you shall forthwith repair with an armed force to the houses of the Jesuits. You will arrest and seize all of them, and dispatch them within twenty-four hours to Veracruz as prisoners. They will be allowed to take only their prayer books and the clothes on their backs. Nothing else will be removed!" Whatever could have happened to cause the king to issue such an order and how could it ever be carried out?

Some background information is necessary to explain the king's earthshaking order. The Jesuits, officially known as The Company Of Jesus, was founded in 1572. They were unique in that they reported directly to the Pope through their Padre Provincial in the new world and their Jesuit General at Rome, by-passing the entire hierarchy of bishops and even the King of Spain himself. The Jesuits were often said to prefer the Papacy to the Monarchy. From the very earliest days of exploration, except for a few Franciscan and Dominican lay brothers, the Jesuits had an exclusive charter to teach Catholicism throughout the new world. There had been a few Franciscan Padres in the new world from 1524, but they labored quietly among the Indians and cared nothing for personal wealth.

The Spanish King had to have the approval of the Jesuit General at Rome before he could appoint governors to his new world provinces, and the Jesuit General even selected the military leaders of New Spain. In reality, all that the king knew about his colonies was what the Jesuits wanted him to know. For many years he had been unable to obtain any real information about what the Jesuits were doing. He had given them orders to treat the Indians fairly and convert them to Christianity, but he was constantly being told that the priests were engaged in enslaving the Indians and becoming wealthy at mining, in direct violation of his orders. King Carlos was also concerned that many of the Jesuits were not Spanish, many of them being German, or from other central European countries.

Before dawn on that fateful day, 3,000 of the king's soldiers marched on the churches and Jesuit houses at Mexico City. At exactly 4 AM the king's order was read at each place where the Jesuits lived. Many wept and a few fainted, but within minutes they were taken from their rooms, possessing nothing but their prayer books and their black robes, all that was allowed for their journey into exile. In the streets one old man tried to speak to a priest and was shot, for no one was allowed to talk to a Jesuit on penalty of death. The arrest of the Jesuits at Mexico City and missions nearby was quickly accomplished, but in the outlying regions, at distant mines and missions, the king's order was not so easily executed.

In order to arrest as many jesuits as possible without warning, a Superior of The Company of Jesus was forced to send a message for all priests throughout each district to gather together at a single mission, where they would receive a written order regarding "a great work to be done for the king." At Sonora and Sinolos 52 Jesuit Priests were arrested and began the long walk to Veracruz. But in Baja and the far reaches of New Mexico it took many weeks and sometimes even months for the soldiers to reach every mission, visita and real of mines, where in many cases only one Jesuit Priest was stationed. At many such places the priest had trusted Indian runners who brought him word of the soldier's approach long before they arrived. There were probably even a few isolated missions unknown to the soldiers, or others which couldn't be located or were overlooked.

One Jesuit Priest at a California mission had sufficient advance warning of his pending arrest to have his mission treasure loaded aboard the ship Dromio. The contraband was intercepted, however, and was reported to be valued at "120,000 pesos in silver, 40,000 pesos in gold plate, 100,000 pesos worth of pearls and 1,000,000 pesos worth of fine furs." It was said that as much as $400,000 in pearls was harvested in one season at his mission. But the good father was arrested and upon his arrival at Seville he languished in a prison until the king's sentence was given, at which time he was beheaded!

After the Jesuit expulsion of 1767, many padres buried their mission treasures.

A mission treasure which has long remained a mystery is that of the lost bells of Tumacacori Mission. The bell tower of the old mission, built during the early 1690s by Father Kino, once held four of the finest bells in all New Spain, but when the Franciscan Padres arrived after the expulsion of the Jesuits, the bells were missing. The expelled Jesuit Priest, Father Alonzo Espinosa, was questioned and freely admitted that he had the bells taken down and buried in the desert close by, but no amount of "persuasion" could make him tell where. The bells would be a real treasure if they could be found, for they were cast of the finest silver-copper alloy especially for the King in 1467, even before the time of Columbus. They were brought from Spain at the special request of Father Kino, so that their silver chimes would call the faithful to worship. The Indians nearby have a legend that during the night, if you listen closely, you may hear the chimes of the lost bells of Tumacacori. It's only a legend, but the old mission belfry does have a place where four bells once hung, but there are no bells there now. Perhaps, if you listen closely. . . .

Even more intriguing is the tale of treasure dug from the mines of Tumacacori and hidden only hours before the Jesuits were seized and forced from their mission. More than a century after the expulsion, records of the mission were uncovered in Spain by Don Santiago Diaz, Governor of Baja, California. They revealed that a king's ransom had been dug from the mines of the Virgin Guadalupe and the Pure Conception, and that a huge hoard of smelted bars of silver and gold had been cached in the concealed tunnels. The portals of both mines were hidden by a rock slide caved down over them when an Indian runner warned the mission priests of the approach of the king's soldiers.

Many have searched for the lost mission treasure, but without the records and waybill found by Governor Diaz their search was in vain, for unknown to them, there were two Tumacacori missions. The ruins of the mission which is today a national monument, where treasure hunting is forbidden, are actually those of the second mission built. Few now know where the original mission was located. Father Kino arrived in Sonora in 1687 and began work on the present mission about 1691. No doubt he chose to build a new mission on the east side of the Santa Cruz River rather than rebuild the original, which had been destroyed during an Indian uprising in 1648. Better agricultural lands were to be had at the new site, since the original mission, located on the west side of the Santa Cruz was on the slopes of the Sierrita Mountains, close by the famed virgin of

Guadalupe and Pure Conception mines, 25 miles northwest of the present national monument.

There are many ancient mine workings in the Sierritas, but the location of the rich mission mines remains a mystery, even through Governor Diaz discovered a waybill giving exact directions to them. The problem is that the waybill is written in archaic Spanish, which nearly all who have tried to solve its riddle have translated it differently. Perhaps you may do better. The basic translation of the waybill is as follows:

"The mine named Guadalupe belongs to Tumacacori. It measures one league from the door of the mission to the southwest, and from the waters of San Roman it is 1,800 varas to the north. 200 varas before arriving at the mine there is a black rock, marked with a cross on its bottom side. 50 varas south from the Cross of Christ will be found buried slabs of silver weighing 250 pounds each. 200 varas to the southwest the rocks of two peaks were caved down by gunpowder, concealing all sign of the mines so that you cannot see them. Inside the mine of Guadalupe are 2,650 jack loads of virgin silver and 905 loads of gold and silver. From the Guadalupe Mine it is 3 leagues to the Pure Conception, the name of which is cut into the stone above the tunnel. The crown, chalices and all of the treasure belonging to Tumacacori were placed in this mine. The metal of the mine is yellow, and half silver and one-fifth gold. The entrance is covered by an iron door with copper handles. The treasure contains 40 millions and is marked in the work book of the mission." If you can solve the enigma of the Jesuit waybill, the

Redotero— Año MDXCVIII–MDCLVIII.- este Redotero pertenecea Temacacury: la Mina de Temacacury.
llamada la Vigen d. Guadalupe. esta una legua medina comensando de la puerta Mayor del Templo al Sr. y de la
agua de San Roman mide a la Siniestra M. ochocientas Vrs al N. y como CCOTO Vrs. antes de llegar a la Mina hay una piedra
negra macada con Cincel con estas marcas por debajo de la piedra est. T.D. = " " de la ɫ esta el Tesoro esto significa
las Letras, y como a XX.- Vrs. de la Piedra adelante, esta un Monumento chico rumbo al Sr. alPnt. de la Mina
hay dos picachos que fueron derrumbados Sobre la Mina sin mas auada que puesta la Polvora en las
rajaduras de las piedras, quedo la hueya borrada para siempre pasando por sobre las piedras no se sabe
donde-esta este lugar dentro de la Mina esta un Patio que mide L. Vrs. en cuadro y en este lugar
esta el Tesoro de nuestras Misiones, en medio del " " esta la boca de la Mina adentro y fuera quedo
el Tesoro: estan MMDCL. Cgs. de plata Sellada y DCCCCV. de oro y plata que son XL.
millones. el oro fue traido de la Siera de Guachapa de las sercanias de Tubaca: seguid
adelante en la misma direcion del Sur.)

Como a III. leguas de la Mina de nestra Sra. de Guadalupe hay I. Puerto que se llama de los Janos
rumbo al S. de aqui sale I. arrollo y desemboca al Rio de Sta. Cruz, la Mina esta a la sinestra del Puerto
abajo del Puerto hay XII. rastras y XII. patios. la Mina tiene I. Tonel de tres cientas Vrs. de largo y el Tonel
tiene el nombre de la Puricima Concepcion gravad, con cincel el Tonel corre al N. y a XX. Vrs. tiene I. tonelito de
cien Varas, al Pr̃e. el metal es amarillo metal que tiene mita de plata y quinta parte de oro hay unos seniceros
cincuenta Vrs. de la puerta de la Mina al rumbo del N. se encontraron planchas de plata virgen
desde una libra hata V. @1 esta = 1= esta tapada con una puerta de cobre tiene unos enormes aldabones
este Cobre fue traido de la Siera de Guachapa de las cercanillas de Tubaca y fundido en Toma-
=cacury y == llevada la prta. en I. rastra, con Buelles a la Mina. Año MDXLVIII. se trabajo y se tapo
en— MDCXLVIII como marca el libro del trabajo de la mision.

De la Mina de la Purima Concepcion a la Mina d. Ntra. Sra. de Guadalupe hay III. leguas como a la mita
del camino a la misma direccion esta la Mina llamada de los Opates – esta tiene I. tonel de cuatro=
=cientas Vrs. y al S. en la misma direccion los metales son calichosos y desde trescietas Vrs se
cortaba con tajadora y de la boca de la Mina corre u. mesa muy larga para la salida del Sol al lado del Pr̃e.
hay I. cañon muy grande y tiene una marca de barreno qe. tiene media Vrs. de ondura parandose al lado
del Sur. se ve la marca al otro lado del cañon rumbo al N. de esta marca hay I. legua a la Mina de los
Opates de Tomacacury. esta la mak. para Pre. al otro lado de la sierra esta la Mina de Ntra. Sra. de
Guadpe esta marcado por P.S.R. el XII del mes de Dcbr. de MDXVIII. fue allada eta Mina por un mi=

Solve the mystery of this ancient Jesuit waybill and find the lost treasure of Tumacacori Mission.

treasure of Tumacacori should be well worth looking for.

Many of the Jesuits were old and didn't survive the long march to Veracruz. Records tell that at least 20 priests from the northern mines died in the Sonoran Desert before reaching Guadalajara, while others were killed by their captors, reportedly while they were being forced to tell where their mission treasures were cached. Others died in prison at Veracruz, aboard ship while en route to Spain or in jails at Seville and Madrid. None were ever allowed to return to the mines and missions they had left behind, or to the countless treasures and caches they concealed before their arrests. The Jesuits in the new world were never many in number. At the time of their expulsion their ranks contained only 418 priests, 678 padres, 123 lay brothers and 137 students in training. Their expulsion forced the closing of 133 missions, 24 colleges and 11 seminaries plus a large number of Indian schools.

Almost immediately tales of Jesuit treasure surfaced, but those which told of concealed treasures almost anywhere in old Mexico might be suspect, for the execution of the king's order was so swift that few prists there had time to bury or conceal anything. But in the distant places of California and the far away mines and missions of New Mexico there was time a plenty to hide both church and personal wealth, while bars of bullion could be cached and mine openings covered or concealed. The Jesuits knew they would never return, so they refused to tell the locations of their hidden treasures, even through torture and death. But many clever maps with strange signs and markings were drawn, and waybills with mysterious codes and cryptic meanings were made. They were hidden under church altars, in secret wall compartments, buried under lone trees, odd shaped rocks or other peculiar landmarks, but probably most often they were sent by trusted Indians to family members, friends or known miners or traders.

Many maps or waybills never reached those intended to receive them, or found their way into mission records or civil archives where they were "lost" for many years. And many of those who did receive maps or waybills couldn't understand them, and even fewer could afford to journey to those

The Jesuits hid many treasures, most still wait to be found.

distant places to conduct searches. Travel into the mountains without a permit was illegal, and those who received maps or waybills dared not confide in the Franciscans or civil officials sent to replace the Jesuits, for they were the very persons who caused the Jesuits to be arrested and imprisoned. It took many years before most maps and waybills began to appear, and then usually in the hands of those who couldn't decipher their obscure meaning. With the Franciscans and the king's soldiers keeping close watch over the old trails north, it was a long time before any searches began.

With the removal of the Jesuits and the coming of the gray-robed Franciscans, it was thought that Christianity, not gold, would be the only purpose for anyone journeying into the far north, but in reality there was no way to keep miners, slavers and adventurers from going into the Great Basin or even as far north as the British possessions. A new map drawn in 1768 by Antonio y Ramirez for the Viceroy of New Spain still showed the San Bueneventura River draining Lake Copalla (On the map Utah Lake and the Great Salt Lake were shown as one) to the Pacific, into a bay Ramirez called Puerto de San Pablo. But if the Franciscans were not interested in gold, they were probably the only Spaniards who were not, as was noted by the English explorer Jonathan Carver a year after the Jesuit expulsion. He described mule caravans bringing silver from mines beyond the Colorado River to Galveston Bay, stating they were so richly laden "that even the shoes of the mules were made of silver!"

During the Jesuit's crisis, France had ceded Louisiana, all of the land west of the Mississippi River, to Spain. A new viceroy had also been inaugurated, Father Teodoro de Croix. While the administration of most viceroys and governors were short lived, Father de Croix's tenure would be a long and impressive one. One of his first actions was to warn the king that he suspected another Indian rebellion was at hand. Indian depridations had become so bad that he reported 1,674 Spaniards had been murdered, and 154 captured and presumably being used as slaves. The Spanish had been forced to abandon 116 haciendas while 68,256 head of livestock had been stolen.

The king responded by granting Viceroy de Croix the additional title of Captain-General, the same rank held by Coronado, with orders to investigate and stop the Indian depridations. The king also reiterated his ban on trading with the Utes without a license from the viceroy. Governor Pedro de Mendinveta echoed the king's order by issuing his own prohibition against venturing into Ute country without a permit.

Viceroy de Croix was placed in charge of all the northern frontier as far north as the Hudson's Bay Company, to protect all of the mines and missions there. He established military detachments known as Presidial Troops and ordered that all parties going into Ute country and all bullion pack trains coming from the mountains would be protected by them. He also directed that for their safety, all mining camps must have at least 24 families assigned to them. His orders were well intentioned, but proved to be impractical. The viceroy informed the king that he had ordered such things "because the king has been spending large sums on troops who can hardly defend themselves, and can do nothing to protect the miners, from whom the King's income comes."

He deplored the status of both his troops and the quality of miners. "Funds sent to pay the troops have been kept by their superiors, their equipment has been in disrepair and some of their weapons will not function. Traders have charged such high prices that the soldiers have become demoralized or insubordinate, and many have deserted for the better pay of mining. In the north our principle incentive is the discovery of silver mines. In the past trained men have been brought from Spain to conduct the operations, but their places have been taken by condemned prisioners, mestizos who know only the work of the hacienda or Indians seized on the complaint that they are cannibals." Unfortunately Viceroy de Croix's plans to improve his military in time proved to be in vain.

During his two expeditions in search of the Indian Wolfskin, Father Rivera had passed by several rich Spanish mines and he was told of even richer prospects in the mountains beyond. Ten years later, in 1775, one of his guides, Gregorio Sandoval, a man who had already made many trips into the far north, led a private party in search of the mines Wolfskin had told Rivera of. Accompanying Sandoval was Andres Muniz, also of the Rivera party, Pedro Mora and several others. They followed Rivera's trail to the crossing of the Colorado at Moab, where they turned north to the Book Cliffs and the Uinta Basin. They discovered some good ore veins and developed at least one mine in the mountains beyond, but the few lines found in old records to describe their journey are too brief to determine exactly where they were.

During the same period many other similar mining parties explored the deserts and ranges between the Great Salt Lake and Boise Basin to the north, and eastward into Wyoming. A few penetrated the discouraging waste lands of the Great Salt Desert to explore the Ruby Mountains, where legend tells a rich mine was worked near present day Harrison Pass. But like the Sandoval party, little is known of their route or where they worked, except for a few names and the dates they departed or returned, and in some cases the date they were arrested for entering the country illegally.

That many brought cargas of gold and silver bullion from the mountains is well known, but the trails they made are too old and dim to follow now. But only one year later, in 1776, the best documented party ever to explore Utah Valley, the ancient land of Teguayo, left Santa Fe following the Old Spanish Trail north. The Dominguez-

Escalante party left such a detailed account of their travels that many earlier and equally important expeditions have been forgotten. Many of the landmarks they described are still known by the same names they gave them.

CHAPTER FOURTEEN

THE ESCALANTE EXPEDITION

"He brought them forth alos with silver and gold."

—Bible, Psalms 105:37

The Dominguez-Escalante expedition left Santa Fe on July 29th, 1776, under the leadership of Fray Francisco Atanasio Dominguez; however, Fray Francisco Silvestre Velez de Escalante accompanied the party as its chronicler or diarist, and because the day-by-day record of its journey was recorded by him, the party is now usually recalled as the Escalante expedition. Don Bernardo Miera went along as a map maker, Andres and Lucrecio Muniz of the Rivera expedition were the parties' guides while others included Don Juan Cisneros, Don Joaquin Lain, Lorenzo Olivares, Juan de Aguilor, Simon Lucero and several Indian servants and guides. The stated purpose of the expedition was to extend one of the west-bound forks of the Old Spanish Trail beyond the Virgin River and Las Vegas Springs to Mission Monterey in California. Escalante also had high hope of establishing a mission among the Indians at Utah Lake, and although their goals were supposed to be Christian in every respect, nevertheless, it soon became evident that several of the party were more interested in mines, especially Don Miera the mapmaker and the Muniz brothers.

The great expedition was hardly started when Miera recorded that near the San Juan River "there still remain ruins of many large and ancient Indian settlements, and furnaces where they apparently melted metals." Their trail passed by the old San Gabriel Mission at the forks of the Chama River, and by the outpost settlement of Abique into Colorado and the Rio Dolores. They made camp on the Utah-Colorado border at Aqua Escondida, where they turned eastward and then north where they passed by the ancient Mt. Hesperous mines visited by Rivera in 1761. From the mines they travelled northwest to Camp Arroyo del Cibolo, near present day Jensen, Utah. From there they followed a well worn trail which had been used by miners and traders for many years, chosen because of its easy terrain and natural mountain passes. Escalante made it abundantly clear that they were

not pathfinders, but were following a well blazed trail, noting "We are following the Ute Trail" or "This is the old slave route." There is no doubt that their route had been in almost constant use for a very long time.

Even greater proof that Escalante was aware of earlier expeditions into the northern reaches of the Great Basin is revealed in his letter to Governor Don Pedro Fermin de Mendinneta on October 28th, 1775, written prior to the Dominguez-Escalante expedition. In it he described how he had learned of earlier Spaniards who had explored and prospected beyond, or west of, the Rio Tizon, the Colorado, long before, "more than forty years since." Escalante noted that that earlier party had been mentioned in the writings of Father Fernando Consag in 1751, their actual explorations into Teguayo being even before that early date. He speculated that they had not travelled north from New Mexico but had made their way from the Pacific coast, "from some ship or other contingency near Monterrey, and had established themselves west of the Rio Tizon." Since the Spanish settlements on the Pacific Coast were on approximately the same latitude as was Santa Fe, Escalante supposed that those early explorers may have been travelling eastward to the settlements of New Mexico. He wrote that if he could locate those unknown Spanish settlements somewhere in Teguayo, west of the Rio Tizon, "their discovery would be very useful to both the church and the Crown."

Both Dominguez and Escalante also knew that the Muniz brothers had made earlier trips to Utah Valley and that they carried a map of that region. Escalante wrote of the Muniz brothers: "They feared disciplining the Utes lest we lose the ancient friendship which they have maintained with them through their vile commerce in pelts, for they have previously been in the habit of staying among the Utes for months at a time, motivated by their greed for peltry." Note that Escalante refers to the "ancient friendship," hardly a term he would have used had he believed he was the first to enter the northern mountains. He also acknowledged that the brothers had previously stayed with the Utes "for months at a time." Another reference was made to earlier explorers when in describing the Las Animas River he wrote, "It flows through a canyon in which there are veins of metal. Although many years ago several persons were sent to investigate and carry away some ore, but it was not learned what metal it was. The Indians and some citizens of this Kingdom said they were silver mines, which caused these mountains to be called Sierra de la Plata."

It is interesting to note how frequently Escalante referred to mines and minerals. On August 11th Muniz told him of a ledge of gold not far from the trail, which they intended to inspect had not Father Dominguez become ill. Escalante

recorded, "Because Father Dominguez was sick we were unable to inspect the veins of metallic rocks in the nearby sierra." While near the Dolores River he described "some mines of transparent and very good gypsum" and again on September 9th observed that "On the side of the canyon there is exposed a vein of metallic ore, but we are ignorant of its nature or quality, although Don Miera says it is of the sort which miners call Tepustite, and that it is an indication of gold ore."

The expedition made its next camp on the east side of the Green River, historically the boundary between the Yutah and Commanche nations since ancient times. Here Escalante made mention of and verifies Fray Alonzo de Posada's journey into the Uinta Mountains and Utah Valley during the period 1660-1664, when he noted, "The Rio de San Bueneventura is the largest river we have yet come to, and is the same which Fray Posada described in

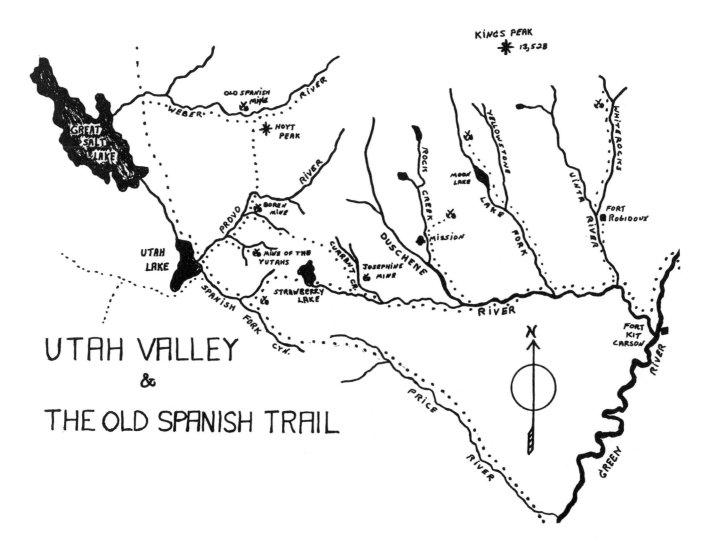

UTAH VALLEY
&
THE OLD SPANISH TRAIL

his report to the King in 1678. According to his record we find it to be the same distance which he places it from Santa Fe." What better evidence could there be that Fray Posada had in fact explored northward into the present day Uinta Basin and on to Utah Valley, or that the Dominguez-Escalante expedition was following the old trail he had blazed more than a century before?

From La Vega de Santa Cruz, their camp on the Green River, the party travelled southwest to the Rio de San Cosme, now the Duchesne River, which they followed past El Canon de los Golondrinas, Red Creek, to Valle de la Pauisma, today's Strawberry Valley. Only some 40 miles north of Escalante's Rio de San Cosme, near present Duchesne, Utah, were the ruins of the Jesuit's Rock Creek Mission. Whether he was unaware of its site or had no interest in going so far out of his way to visit another sect's failure is unknown. At any rate he never mentioned it.

At Strawberry Valley they turned to the southwest down the steep Rio San Lino, now Diamond Creek, into Spanish Fork Canyon, which name had been in use long before their arrival. Many other Spanish names sometimes attributed to Escalante were in common use long before their expedition, including the Sierra de la Sal and Abajo mountains, the San Rafael River and Desert, the San Juan River and the Wasatch (Guasvates) Mountains. Escalante named the Spanish Fork River, Rio de Aqua Calientas for the hot springs found along its course. On September 23rd, 1776, they entered into the large valley which had long been known to Spanish explorers as Teguayo, and looked upon its great fresh water lake, the legendary Lake Copalla.

Escalante named the valley Nuestra Senora de la Merced de Timpanocutzis, which he noted was surrounded by high peaks and had a lake "six leagues wide and 15 leagues long," with four rivers running into it. He named the lake Laguna de Timpanocutzis. His Timpanocutzis is now spelled Timpanogos, while the lake has become Utah Lake. Whether or not Escalante intended it, Timpanocutzis is an Aztec word meaning "the stone person." 12,000' Mt. Timpanogos, which towers above the lake and valley below, bears the outline of a sleeping maiden, or a "stone person." He also gave names to the three rivers north of the

Rio de Aqua Calientes. First was Rio de San Nicolas, now Hobble Creek, Rio San Antonio de Padua, now the Provo River and Rio de Santa Ana, now the American Fork River.

Don Miera, the mapmaker, also kept a detailed derrotero, or diary, in which he wrote that Utah Valley was the choicest place he had yet seen. "Several presidios and missions should be established here, the principle one at the Lake of Timpanocutzis or on one of the rivers which flow into it, for this is the most pleasing, beautiful and fertile spot in all New Mexico." Apparently Escalante agreed, for in his official report he added, "The sierras towards the east are likewise very fertile, having many rivers and springs, and timber, including royal and other pines." Nor did he overlook the possibility of nearby mines, for he continued, "The veins which are seen in the sierras appear from a distance to have minerals."

Miera left an even more intriguing tale of gold mines not far from Utah Lake. "The Timpanocutzis Indians say that the tribes living up on high ridges of the sierras which can be seen from their houses were formerly their friends, and that they make the tips of their arrows and lances and also of their macranos (war clubs) of a yellow metal in accordance with ancient traditions." That reference became especially interesting when it later became known that in the mountains just beyond Utah Lake there were such fabulous places as the Lost Mine Of The Yutahs, a hieroglyphic mine in Daniel's Canyon and the famed Josephine Mine on Currant Creek in addition to the several Lost Rhoades Mines of the Uinta Basin.

Because it was so late in the season, fresh snow already dusting the top of Mt. Timpanocutzis, Father Dominguez started his little party towards the southwest, still hoping to reach Monterey Mission before winter closed the high passes. Both Escalante and Don Miera promised the Utes that they would return to establish a mission at Utah Lake. They followed the Sevier River, their Rio de Santa Isabel, to Sevier Lake, where Rivera had explored fifteen years before. Sevier Lake was then much larger than it is today, and they named it Laguna de Miera. Don Miera still believed the Sevier and the Green were the same rivers, and he so outlined it on his map. In his derrotero he wrote, "The San Bueneventura River is the same Rio del

Tizon discovered by Juan de Onate in 1598," and on his map he showed it flowing westward across present Nevada to the Sierra Nevadas. Later mapmakers extended it to the Pacific, perpetuating his error. Of course Miera was mistaken, but he does suggest that some of Onate's party may have ventured as far north as the Sevier River.

On October 3rd they passed by the desolate Crickett Hills, where a century later a huge cache of gold would be found, and then lost again. There their Indian guide Jose Maria deserted them, and with winter fast approaching, the decision to return to Santa Fe was made. They continued south to Ash Creek and the Virgin River, into the beautiful but desolate wastelands of southern Utah. But even there Mierra still thought of treasure when he wrote that they had crossed "a deep canyon where there is a large amount of copperas." At Ash Creek Escalante recorded, "All the land is poor, although it appears to be rich in minerals. Along the river there are ash heaps, veins and signs of minerals and many stones of reddish mica and chalchihvite, a greenish stone."

With the greatest difficulty they made their way down to the Colorado River which they forded at the Crossing Of The Fathers. From there they travelled southeast to where they picked up Pedro de Tovar's trail of 1540, which they followed back to Santa Fe, arriving there on January 2nd, 1777. Escalante closed his report by writing, "Everything contained herein is true and faithful to what occurred and was observed during our journey, which we do sign on the 3rd day of January, 1777."

Not long afterwards Don Miera submitted his own report to the king, apparently in the hope that he would receive permission to lead his own expedition back to Utah Lake. After describing the many veins of minerals found in the sierras, he wrote that the Utes were now so strong and well armed that there was danger of the Spanish being driven from the mountains again. "For so fierce are their attacks and so great the consternation they cause, that many of the settlements on those frontiers have been abandoned, and all mining stopped, thus reducing the Royal income and multiplying the cost of troops. I promise Your Majesty, God giving me life and health, that in the term of three years with the troops I have requested, to give peace and quiet to that province, and to have three settlements established and to have at least one mine of gold, silver and copper discovered and working."

Whether or not the king was impressed with Miera's report, the following year he did encourage mining again, but in deference to Escalante's report he directed that the Indians should be won over by gentle means and not by force. He also reemphasized his ban against unlicensed traders going into the land of the Utes. The new trade ban, dated September 13th, 1778, had as its main purpose the control of firearms being sold or traded to the Utes, but in many cases the Utes were already better armed than the Spaniards, obtaining many firearms and other contraband from the French traders who came from the north.

Quite unexpectedly Spain declared war on England less than a year later, so there were no new troops dispatched to defend the northern borderlands, and Don Miera never got the army he requested. Once more the miners and traders were on their own, with little control over the places they went or record of the mines they worked or the Indians they seized as slaves. Only two years later French fur trappers reported seeing long pack trains loaded with silver bullion coming from the northern mountains. The pack trains were so rich they said, "That even the trappings on the horses were made of pure silver!"

CHAPTER FIFTEEN

THE COMING OF THE AMERICANS

"There's gold, and it's haunting and haunting;
It's luring me on as of old;
Yet it isn't the gold that I'm wanting,
So much as just finding the gold."

— Robert Service

The return of Escalante to Santa Fe and the subsequent release of both his and Don Miera's reports to the king greatly encouraged the return of mining parties to the northern frontier. Copies of Miera's map were in great demand, used by miners and traders in the furtherest reaches of the relatively unknown western deserts and the remote peaks of the distant mountains. New mines were discovered and old ones concealed by the Indians after the revolt of 1680 were reopened. A few were found using Jesuit maps or waybills secretly made during the revolt.

When the Jesuits were arrested, frequently a hurriedly drawn map or scribbled waybill was hidden in some secret place, often not found until many years later. They were difficult to decipher, for place names used by the padres had changed or were unknown to their finders, and even the length of a vara or a league had changed over the years. In less than one hundred years the league shrunk from 3.45 to 2.52 miles.

One waybill preserved by a pioneer family at Utah Valley read as follows: "Follow the river into the sierra beyond its first fork, where you will find two barren and rocky peaks close by each other. There is a mine below the pass between them, facing towards the setting sun. Look for three large royal pines standing wide apart from each other, and directly in front of them you will find three flat stones. These stones can be distinguished by a large cross cut on the center stone with an iron bar. The opening to the mine is between the three trees and the stones. It is covered by a large flat stone which was placed over it by 25 Indians using levers. As you enter the mine you will find golden images, vases, monstrances and many other precious things. When you descend the shaft you will find four stacks of silver bars and other objects of great value." There are several locations which answer

that general description, and at one an old shaft has been discovered, but it is so badly caved that it may never be opened. Only time will tell what is hidden in its depths.

The resurgence of mining increased the demand for Indian slaves to work at the mines. Fray Juan Augustin de Morfi wrote to Viceroy de Croix protesting their harsh treatment, and once more the viceroy warned that another Indian revolt was imminent. His letter warned that the French were ready and anxious to claim the Spanish borderlands. "I am persuaded that if we lose the barrier of the northern province, which I pray to God will not happen, the Indians would quickly seize all of that immense land, while the French, accustomed as they are to living by robbery, would undoubtedly approach us." De Croix's letter also reported that with the Spanish soldiers diverted by the war in Europe, the soldiers of New Mexico were in a sad state of readiness. "They know nothing of discipline, they lose their horses, they are not skilled with firearms, have no uniforms and are frequently hungry. The great distances between the mines and missions in the north makes it very easy for the Indians to avoid the troops." But the king had no troops to send, and besides, there was more gold and silver coming from the mountains than ever before.

It was impossible for the viceroy's few soldiers to police the entire frontier, but still a few unlicensed traders or slavers were arrested. In 1783 a party of ten Spaniards was arrested for illegal trade with the Utes, and in 1785 five more were arrested "For trading in the interior in violation of repeated edicts." They were fined by Governor Juan Bautists de Anza, but they had cached their illicit bullion before being caught, making their work well worth while. Civil records reveal that even as late as 1797 a party of 22 miners was arrested on their return to Abique, for trespassing into Ute territory without a permit. Viceroy de Croix signed a new ten-year peace compact with the Utes in 1777, but only the Ute Chiefs Mora and Pinto acknowledged the treaty, while most other chiefs were unaware of it.

As the new century drew near during the waning years of the 1700s, Spain found an even greater problem to contend with, for the Americans were beginning to push beyond the Rockies and into the Great Basin. They came to trap furs, trade with the Indians, seek for gold and to find their fortunes. In 1785 a party of 20, 14 of them Americans led by Philip Nolen, rode deep into Spanish territory seeking horses. They were attacked by Spanish soldiers and Nolen was killed, with the rest taken as prisoners. They were marched south to Chihuahua where for five long years they languished in a foul prison while waiting the king's sentence. Finally King Charles III directed that every fifth man was to be shot, but by then only nine still survived, so only one was shot and the rest sentenced to ten years at hard labor. Not long afterwards three American traders named McKnight, Chambers and Beard made their way to Taos, a main supply point for the Spanish mines. They were seized as spies and thrown into prison where they remained until after the Mexican revolution in 1821.

One of the first parties of American fur trappers to venture into Spanish territory was led by James Ohio Pattie. Little is known of their travels for it seems Pattie was a better liar than he was a trapper, still others soon followed him. The American trappers and the Mountain Men had little trouble evading the Spanish soldiers, and in many cases they even outnumbered them. Many of the Americans, expecting to find an uninhabited wilderness, were astonished to find well travelled trails, developed trade routes and old mines and missions which had been occupied in the long ago. Some had been abandoned so long brush covered them and trees grew among their ruins. They soon realized that they were only rediscovering frontiers which the Spanish had already claimed and explored for 300 years and more.

Governor Charles Delossus became so alarmed at the incursions of the Americans that he warned, "If the greatest precautions are not taken to stop them, within a short time we will see Americans descending the Missouri River with Spanish furs and silver from Spanish mines!" That the Americans were a real threat was reenforced by French Governor Baron de Carondelet, when he described how an American could live and profit where a Frenchman or Spaniard might starve.

"The 'wandering spirit and ease with which these Americans obtain their sustenance and shelter and quickly form new settlements and states presents a great danger. A rifle and a little maize in a sack are enough for an American to wander about the forests alone for a whole month. With his rifle he kills the wild cattle and deer and defends himself from the savages. The maize, dampened a little, serves him as bread. With a few tree trunks crossed one above another in the shape of a square he raises a house, and even a fort which is impregnable to the savages. The cold does not affect him. When he tires of one location he moves to another, and there settles with the same ease. If such men occupy the shores of the Mississippi and Missouri, there is nothing that can prevent them from penetrating into our provinces, and since these places are still a great part wilderness, it appears that no obstacle can oppose them." His warning was timely, for the days of the French and the Spanish as well were numbered.

Shortly after 1800 Americans were travelling along the Old Spanish Trail. In 1808 a party of trappers led by Workman & Spence made their way to California by following a Spanish trading party along the trail to Fish Lake and the Virgin River. The following year several other Americans were allowed to accompany a party of Spanish traders, taking the trail from Moab on the Colorado across central Utah to the Sevier River and south to California. The Americans first realized how old the Old Spanish Trail was when in 1805 Governor Joaquin de Real Alencaster commended 70 year old Manuel Meastes for his services as an interpreter among the Indians at Utah Valley since 1750. Meastes had been an interpreter for Governor de Anza during his campaign against the Commanches in 1779.

Another well documented trade party which made frequent trips into Utah Valley before the arrrival of the Americans was that of Mauricio Arze and Lagas Garcia. After their last trip north in 1813, they were arrested and returned to Abique for violating the ban on trading with the Utes. They appeared before Alcalde Manuel Garcia at Santa Cruz, and when asked about their route north, stated they had followed the Sevier River into the western part of the territory. The court record indicated that it was a commonly used route, for it states, "The trail northward is so well known that there is no need to expand upon it."

With the increasing commerce, mines lost since the revolt of 1680 were being reopened and worked again. At the ancient Santa Rita Mine pack trains were once more carrying heavy loads of silver south into Mexico. The mine had been well concealed and wouldn't have been found without a map. The miners who rediscovered it found a cache of silver bullion, and the place where the bars had been poured. A mold consisting of four cavities, each 6"x20" in size, was cut into the flat sandstone rock close to a smelter site where the bullion had been melted. After the mine's discovery, Dionissio Robles, with a large and well-armed party searched north from Santa Rita where they located "an old mine and workings cleverly concealed by the Jesuits." Not long afterwards Robles and his companions were driven from the mountains by Indians. It is unknown whether the "cleverly concealed" mine was ever found again.

Leather shoulder ore packs found deep inside the ancient Santa Rita Mine.

In 1765 Father Rivera had been told by friendly Utes that in the mountains far to the north of Spanish Valley there was a settlement of buckskin clothed, bearded men. Besides the tale told to Rivera, there are several other accounts of a "lost" mining camp or mission in the mountains separating Utah and Wyoming. That such a "lost" settlement existed is confirmed by an 1811 expedition in which Jose Rafael Sarracino was sent with a small guard of soldiers to search for such a settlement. Indians near Moab told him they knew of such a place in the mountains north and west of the Green River. Sarracino spent the remainder of summer seeking the settlement to no avail, but he reported he had come near it, for he found "many things among the Indians traded or stolen from the miners, such as knifes and awls. The Indians say they were given these things by men who live in stone houses by a stream near where they dig for silver." Could Sarracino have been seeking one of the mission settlements established by Villasur soon after 1700?

1810 marked the beginning of the end of Spanish occupation in the west. In September of that year Father Miguel Hidalgo urged the Indians, mestizos and genizaros, the peons and the enslaved, the Mexicans, to rebell against Spanish rule. It was to be a long, hard and bloody fight, but after eleven years the Mexicans won their independence from Spain. Many things occurred during these hard years. Spain was forced to pull its soldiers out of the north, abandoning most of its western territory to the Americans. Without the protection of soldiers, hundreds of mines and dozens of missions were abandoned, and countless treasure caches were hidden until the miners, soldiers and padres could return for them. But they never returned, for with Mexican independence in 1821, Spain could no longer lay claim to the American west, so the treasures they hid are still hidden, right where they cached them.

It took only a few short years for the Americans to claim all of the land it had taken Spain 300 years to acquire. And although the Spanish had taken millions of dollars from the land in gold and silver, millions more still remained, much of it hidden at crumbling missions, concealed in covered mine shafts and tunnels or buried in secret caches. It was a time for legends and treasure tales.

One of the first treasure legends given birth by the Mexican Revolution was born only a few months after the overthrow of the Spanish began. A strange tale is told of an even stranger treasure buried in a shallow cave near the north end of the Kaiparowits Plateau, close to the little town of Escalante in Garfield County, Utah. When the revolution began in 1810, Indians aided by a few sympathetic mestizos joined to set fire to a mission and drive its padre and soldier guards from the land. The padre had been a mine owner whose mission had acquired great wealth at the expense of many Indian lives. With his few soldiers to assist him, he loaded 20 burros with gold artifacts from the mission and silver bullion from his mine. They fled north to avoid the Apaches who were raiding Spanish settlements to the south. From the mine, according to some located near the Virgin River Gorge, they followed the north side of the Colorado River, hoping to reach the Old Spanish Trail and escape along it to Santa Fe.

Their pursuers were persistent, however, and every day saw several of the heavily laden burros fall to exhaustion, or another soldier killed by Indians who pursued them. When they reached the north end of the Kaiparowits Plateau, known locally as the Fifty Mile Mountain, they realized they could never hope to cross the waterless desert which lay ahead without being caught and all of them killed. With the threat of death very real, the padre and his last two soldiers decided that their only chance was to cache their heavy treasure. In a shallow cave in the black malpais rock they hid the heavy bars of bullion and all of the church treasure, including the Golden Jesus, a three foot high cross of solid gold bearing a figure of the crucified Christ on it. The cross was so heavy that it took all three of them to lift it. After all of their treasure was hidden, the small cave was covered over with pieces of stone. All expected that one day they would return, but unknown to them, the land would never be under Spanish control again.

The legend of the Golden Jesus might be treated as just another treasure tale, except for what happened 60 years later. By the 1870s Mormon pioneers had settled much of southern Utah, and many heard Indians tell of the running fight so long before, and they heard strange tales of a cave in the mountains from which Indians sometimes brought Catholic crosses, gold chains and silver goblets to trade for food. Bishop Llewellen Harris had been especially kind to the impoverished Indians, and in return for his kindness one of them told him how to find the cave. But in those hard days of settling the desert, Bishop Harris had no time to explore the rugged Fifty Mile Mountain, so several years passed before he made any search.

He never found the cave of the Golden Jesus, but he did find the bones of burros and the frames of pack saddles, and atop the plateau he found an old Spanish spur and part of a broken sword. Even today an occasional hunter or a cowboy finds an ancient looking hand-forged mule shoe, or the brass button from a soldier's uniform. If you should stop while at Escalante, almost anyone can point out the trail to Fifty Mile Mountain, and there are still a few old-timers who remember the tale of the Golden Jesus.

CHAPTER SIXTEEN
A TIME FOR LEGENDS

*"Stranger tales than these are told,
But none so tempting, true, or bold!"*

—Anonymous

During the long years of the Mexican Revolution, a huge amount of treasure accumulated at mines, missions and at harbors along the gulf coast. Many pack trains of bullion were being brought from the mountains even without the king's soldiers to guard them. But by 1820 it became obvious that Spain couldn't win its war against the combined Indian and Mexican forces, so ships were hurriedly loaded as heavily as their crews dared, and the last plate fleet sailed for Spain. The next year Mexico won its independence and the Spanish domination of the Americas ended. Three hundred years of pillaging and plundering came to an end, but at a terrible cost to the Indians. An estimated twenty billion dollars in gold, silver and turquoise had been stolen and shipped to Spain, then more wealth than existed in all the rest of the world. An even greater price had been paid by the Indians through enslavement. Padre Perez de Ribas had earlier described their fate.

"How was it that our brave Captain-General could keep at relative peace perhaps one hundred thousand Indians with a force of only forty-six Spanish soldiers? He ordered made many heavy iron collars with chains attached. 42 Indians were taken prisoner, 7 of them chiefs, and the iron collars were placed around their necks. Meanwhile he had ordered several large trees prepared for their hanging. At the base of these trees the prisoners were baptized and consoled during their last moments. During this time they were watched closely by a guard in armor. And so they were left hanging, 42 Indians who had been made to tremble in fear of the Christians of the province." It seems ludicrous now to picture 42 Indians being baptized to save their souls from hell while they are waiting to be hung!

The good padre commented further on how the Spanish had decimated the ranks of the Indians. "Due to the inroads of disease and other causes (among them the hangings already described multiplied a thousand times and more) there are not now one-half the number of Indians there were when the Spaniards came to these lands. It is commonly said that their employment in farming, mining and other enterprises had greatly reduced their number, and although it is undoubtedly true that some Spaniards are extreme in their treatment of Indian laborers, this is the exception." By the Spaniard's own records, more than three million Indians became "exceptions."

A little known Colorado treasure in Spanish silver was lost soon after the Mexican Revolution. With the outster of the Spanish, Americans lost no time expanding their own trade with the Indians, and even the towns of Santa Fe and Taos became their outfitting places. One of the first American traders was William Becknell, who in the first months of Mexican independence advertised in the Missouri *Intelligencer* for men to go westward "For the purpose of trading for horses and mules and catching wild animals of every description." In only a few years Becknell became wealthy in his trade among the Indians.

During August, 1828, he completed an especially lucrative trading venture and with a few men began the return to Missouri, carrying $50,000 in Spanish silver reales. Their trail led northeast into Colorado, where they were attacked by Commanche Indians. Their livestock was stolen, and the traders, desperate for water, divided the heavy sacks of silver among them and began struggling northward on foot to the Arkansas River, which they reached near Chauteau's Island, now near present day Granada. There was no possibility of carrying the silver further, so it was cached on or near the island, and the survivors began a desperate 400 mile walk to the nearest settlements in Missouri. Men were killed by Indians or fell exhausted and died of thirst all along the way. Only 15 miles from the frontier settlement of Independence the last man crawled into a farm clearing, "blinded by starvation and fighting off wolves with a stick." He alone knew where the treasure was cached, but blind and close to death he could not lead his rescuers back across 400 miles of Commanche country to it. So it still waits to be found, $50,000 in Spanish silver, worth a hundred times that much today.

Each passing year saw hundreds and then thousands of traders and fur trappers traversing their newly won west, and in their journals and diaries many commented on the ruins of forts, missions and settlements they came upon, and the old mine workings so long abandoned. In the American vocabulary the word Spanish was quickly replaced by the name Mexican, and after the arrival of the Mountain Men, the old ruins and mines found were almost always described as being Mexican. Probably the last Spanish-Mexican pack train to travel the Old Spanish Trail was one led by Governor Antonio Armijo in 1829. It was followed closely by the first American traders, led by William Wolfskill. Almost as if the Americans were destined to continue the Spanish tradition of mining, that very first American trading party discovered gold at the edge of the mountains.

The Fish Lake section of the old trail followed by Wolfskill, George Yount, Lewis Burton and several others late in 1830 crossed the headwaters of the Sevier and Virgin Rivers to the Little Salt Lake, north of present day Summit in Iron County. In a blinding snowstorm they sought refuge in the mouth of nearby Winn Canyon. The storm proved to be one of the winter's worst, so cold their horses froze to death. For days they burned cedar trees to keep from freezing, and thawed frozen horse flesh for food. In his journal Wolfskill wrote what must be considered one of the greatest understatements of all time: "It is a cheerless prospect, calculated to cause emotions by no means agreeable to even the stoutest heart!"

While searching for fire wood, the traders discovered a ledge of gold, but stranded in a mountain blizzard far from either Santa Fe or the missions of California, the gold held little interest for them. But of no immediate use, they no doubt intended to return for it, for they left a cryptic message cut into a black volcanic boulder at the mouth of Winn Canyon. Incribed onto the rock is the message.

"Gold 1831," with the initials "W," "LB," and "Y," initials of the party's leaders. Eventually most of the traders reached Monterey where both Wolfskill and Yount claimed large tracts of land and became wealthy, with no need to ever return to their starvation camp at Winn Canyon. Burton and the others faded into the obscurity of time, and now only the gold remains for some modern day Mountain Man to find.

Gold! 1831. The Wolfskill waybill rock at Winn Canyon. *(Courtesy Utah State Historical Society.)*

At almost the same time, in 1828, Pegleg Smith, one of the West's most colorful characters as well as one of its best for fur trappers led a party along the Old Spanish Trail which found a gold placer not far from Wolfskill's find. Smith, who had amputated his own leg after being shot with a poisoned arrow, with several companions made camp on the Rio Santa Clara at the foot of the Pine Valley Mountains. Dutch John, one of the trappers, looked for beaver sign along the river, but found a bar of rich placer gold instead. He scooped up a hat full of the red colored nuggets and showed them to Smith and the others. The half starved trappers decided the nuggets were native copper, so with little interest in them they broke camp and continued to Las Vegas Springs and

California. But Dutch John took a pocket full of the nuggets with him, and in California he traded them for enough whiskey to stay drunk for a month. The trappers move on to the Oregon country, never returning to the Santa Clara, so the location of Pegleg Smith's placer gold remains just another mystery along the Old Spanish Trail.

Far to the north, in the Uinta Mountains which separate Utah from Wyoming, other traders and trappers were cashing in on the lucrative trade with the Utes. During the early 1830s, Antoine Robidoux, one of a large family of traders from St. Louis, built Fort Robidoux on the Escalante Trail of 1776. It was built on the site of an earlier fort at the forks of the Uintah and Whiterocks River, just south of the present day Indian settlement of Whiterocks. It was only one of three forts built in that northern Ute country at about the same time, the others being Fort Davy Crockett, some 50 miles northeast of Fort Robidoux on the Green River in Brown's Hole and Fort Kit Carson, about 40 miles southeast of Fort Robidoux at the forks of the Green and Duchesne Rivers.

The Robidoux Inscription at Westwater Canyon. "Antoine Robidoux passed here on 13 November 1837 to establish a fort." *(Courtesy Utah State Historical Society.)*

All three forts became trade centers for American fur trappers and supply points for many of the old Spanish mines then being found in the Uinta Mountains. Under the Mexicans who worked many of the mines, slavery became equally as vicious as it had been under the Spanish. In 1842 "Old Joe" Williams, a Methodist preacher turned fur trapper, described the sad lot of both Indians and Mexicans at Fort Robidoux. "I am appalled by the wickedness of those trading here, with their swearing, drinking and debauchery of the Indians. They are dirty, fat and idle!" But unsuspected by Robidoux or the traders, trappers and miners, an Indian revolt equal in intensity to the great revolt of 1680 was being planned by the Utes, this time to drive both the Mexicans and Americans from the mountains for good, and close the hated mines forever.

Traders like Robidoux were well aware that the Indians had places were they obtained silver or gold but were unable to learn its source, for the Indians had no desire to see more of the Spanish mines reopened. "For years the Indians have been known to possess a secret mine of silver which surpasses in richness anything known to exist. They make rings, bracelets and other ornaments out of pure silver, but when asked where the metal is obtained, only answer with a shrug of the shoulders are a grunt." But with ever more trappers and gold hunder coming into the mountains, a few of the old Spanish mines were being located, one of the richest being El Mina de Perdito Alma, the Mine of Lost Souls.

El Mina de Perdito Alma was found by the use of a Jesuit waybill, reportedly obtained from an old mestizo at Santa Fe by one of the trappers at Fort Robidoux. He traded it to a Mexican for a pack of prime furs. The waybill stated in part, "Follow the Rio San Bueneventura (Green River) to El Sierra Blanca de los Lagunas (Uinta Mountains). Cross the rio and turn to the northeast, following the second arroyo crossing (Ashley Creek) for 14 leagues, to el promontorio de last hundir agujero (promontory of the sink hole). There you will find a cueva (cavern) and just beyond is el mina."

The Mine of Lost Souls was worked in the most primitive fashion; however, Indian labor was plentiful. The Indians were virtual prisoners at the mine until they died or escaped. An American trained in mining described the methods used at the mines of the Uintas near Fort Robidoux. "Without machinery of any kind, using only fire, unslaked lime or sometimes black powder to break the ore, Mexican miners removed thousands of tons of solid rock, at one place for 200' into a shaft and another 100' along the vein. Its removal required countless thousands of loads of rock, all carried out on the backs of Indians. Even more trips were required to pack out the sump water in animal skins. Fiber or cowhide sacks were used to carry the ore while pigskin bags served as water containers. Torches were made of grass and tallow pounded together and the bound tightly with fiber made from cedar bark."

Mines in the Uintas required a never ending supply of Indian labor, but times had changed greatly since the Spanish had worked them, for by the arrival of the Mexicans most Utes had horses and many owned firearms, taken from Spaniards killed or obtained through trade. The mission priests at the scattered mining camps of the Uintas knew that the Indians were on the verge of rebellion, and told them that when the Americans replaced the Mexicans times would be better. But the Indians saw that without change they were doomed to annihilation, and replied that if they were to die, they were determined to die in their own land and with their own beliefs.

In September, 1844, in a rebellion as well planned as the one Pope had organized in 1680, the Utes at all of the mines and missions of the Uinta Mountains rebelled and in one bloody uprising either killed or drove all of the Mexican miners and American traders from the mountains. At the same time others attacked and burned Forts Robidoux, Kit Carson and Davy Crockett. Everything was destroyed, from the simplest visita to the largest mission, including the smallest mining prospect to great mines like El Mina de Perdito Alma. Nearly everyone was killed or driven away, but by chance Robidoux was on a trading trip and escaped their fury.

A legend has grown of the murdered miners at El Mina de Perdito Alma. During the attack, all of the Mexican miners were killed except one old man and his granddaughter, who were away in the nearby hills picking berries. They watched in horror as their friend's bodies were mutilated and thrown into the deep shaft. Because they were not given the last rites of the church, they were "lost souls." Heavy bars of bullion and mining tools were also thrown into the shaft, while the few log and brush huts were burned. Unknown to the Indians, the miners had hidden a great cache of silver bars under one of their cabins.

Many years later an old Mexican woman who had been the young girl picking berries was brought to nearby Vernal by her two sons, to help them locate the old mine and the cache of silver bars buried under one of the cabins. The old woman was nearly blind, but she still recalled that the mine was located on one side of a high promontory of land, not far from a natural cave and close by a sink hole on the river. She also remembered a natural stone bridge downstream from the mine. Her sons made many trips into the mountains, but gave up when winter's snows came.

Today, if you follow Dry Fork Canyon upstream, some four miles west of Vernal, and watch closeely, you will come to a point of land, or a promontory where the creek divides, 17 miles up canyon. Follow the left fork of the creek and you will see a natural stone arch. In some thick brush a half mile further there is a cave, and just beyond it, a sinkhole on the river. It's all there, just as the old Mexican woman said. And the mine is just beyond, somewhere. . . .

Miners were also attacked and their mines destroyed at places like Brush Creek, the Yellowstone, Uintah and Whiterocks Rivers, and further west on Rock Creek, the Duschene and Strawberry Rivers and at Currant Creek. All of them were so cleverly concealed and covered over that few have ever been found. Hardly a trace remains of Fort Robidoux, while only a stone foundation marks the site of Fort Kit Carson. The site of Fort Davy Crockett is now under the waters of Flaming Gorge Lake. Little remains of the old mines of the Uintas, except old trails in the mountains which seem to go nowhere. There is still an occasional discovery of an old Spanish bell or a spur, or the rusted pieces of an antique rifle, or perhaps some hand-forged tool to remind us of the lost mines of the Uintas and the Indian revolt of 1844.

CHAPTER SEVENTEEN
THE MORMONS AND SPANISH MINES

*"Iron made Britain great,
Gold ruined Spain!"*

—Brigham Young

It would be logical to assume that with the coming of the Americans, slavery would be stopped. But from the Mexican Revolution to the arrival of the Mormons in 1847 slavery of the Indians reached its zenith. Since there were no longer any royal bans prohibiting unlicensed parties from going into the northern mountains, more mines were being worked than ever before, and with the increased demand for Indian laborers, slavery increased greatly. Almost every journal or record kept by the fur companies or their trappers mentioned the slave trade. In 1839 Thomas Farnham wrote, "These poor creatures are hunted in the spring of the year when they are weak and helpless, and when captured are carried to Santa Fe where they are sold as slaves." Trapper George Ruxton noted, "Commanches, for the purpose of procuring animals and slaves, carry off young boys and girls, massacring the adults in the most wholesale and barbarous manner. So regular are their slaving expeditions that in the Commanche calendar, the month of September is known as the Mexican Moon."

Dr. J.H. Lyman travelled among the Piutes of western Utah in 1841 and observed: "The Mexicans capture the Pi-Utes for slaves, the neighboring Utes do the same, and even the bold and usually high-minded old beaver hunter sometimes descends from his legitimate labors among the mountain streams to this mean traffic. The price of these slaves at the markets at Santa Fe varies with the age and other qualities of person. Those from 10 to 15 years old fetch from $50 to $100, which is by no means an extravagant price, if we take into consideration the task of cleansing them fit for market!" One had only to follow the slaver's trails to find the Mexican mines where many of the slaves were taken. Those old mines were being reopened from the Grand Canyon to the northern Rockies. Oddly enough, one of them was discovered by a Jesuit Priest!

In 1841 Father Pierre Jean de Smet, a French Jesuit who had journeyed from the Great Lakes region to teach Christianity to the Indians of the Idaho-Wyoming area, discovered the ruins of a very old Jesuit mission in the Big Horn Mountains of Wyoming. Of even greater interest is the fact that he used a Jesuit map of great antiquity, which map accurately portrayed the mountain ranges of northern Utah and Wyoming, even though it had been made long before the Jesuit expulsion of 1767.

Father De Smet found the mission ruins near the shore of a small lake at the headwaters of Piney Creek, north of present Buffalo, Wyoming. That lake is now shown on maps as Lake De Smet. In his report he stated, "These ruins are more than a century old." A history of Wyoming contains the following: "A map prepared by the Jesuits and now preserved in their archives at Paris, contains an accurate sketch of the Black Hills and the Big Horn Mountains. Ruins of stone houses and fortifications, as well as remains of iron tools and old mine workings in the Big Horn Basin give strong proof of early Spanish explorations throughout the state."

Equally as interesting is another old account which states, "In the Wind River Mountains near Lander, Wyoming, some very old 'pictographs' on a ledge represent men wearing striped or slashed apparel, which looks very much like armor. The figures are thought to represent early Spanish travellers. There are also old 'signs' nearby, one of them a snake, as well as other strange symbols. Those familiar with such things say they were made by Spaniards more than 200 years ago to direct the way to a treasure they buried when attacked by Indians."

One might think to dismiss such reports, especially when prestigious historical societies deny there was any Spanish exploration so far north, if they hadn't been verified later. In 1865 General

Patrick E. Conner, while leading his Powder River Expedition from Fort Douglas, Utah, reported seeing the very same ruins that Father De Smet had reported in 1841. General Connor wrote that in his opinion the ruins were very old, more than a century, being built long before the time of Escalante.

An explanation of the Wyoming ruins might be found in a statment made by one Father Ortiz to General Steven Kearney in 1848. When questioned about early explorations, Father Ortiz said that records of his mission revealed that Spanish traders and padres had explored along the San Bueneventura (Green) River as far as 800 miles north of Santa Fe during the early 1600s. They there built a mission where "they lived in stone huts and worked mines close by, milling their ore in arrastras. The Indians rebelled about 1650 and drove them from the mountains." The description given by Father Ortiz resembles very closely the "lost settlement" sought by Jose Sarracino in 1811.

In 1866 the ruins of a very old arrastra was found near Fort Phil Kearney, near the edge of Lake DeSmet, while an old stone chimney believed to be the remnants of a Spanish smelter were located in Slade Canyon, near Fort Laramie. Pieces of slag found at the smelter site were assayed and revealed that a high grade silver ore, also containing some gold, was smelted there. Both of these finds almost certainly explains the discoveries of Father DeSmet and General Connor. Of local interest is the fact that Slade Canyon was named for the notorious outlaw, Jack Slade, who made a dying statement that he had buried a cache of gold coins, jewelry and other robbery loot near the old stone chimney, known locally as "Slade's Chimney." If you're interested in outlaw treasure, you might want to check the story out, for Slade's treasure has never been found!

American military expeditions were responsible for discovering many old Spanish mines, all across the west. Dr. F.A. Wislizenus with the Doniphan Expedition in Arizona in 1848 wrote, "Many now deserted mining places prove that mining was pursued with greater zeal in the old Spanish times than it is at present. These mountains are very rich in gold, copper, iron and silver." Daniel Tyler, an enlisted man with the Mormon Batallion, described a place where ancient arrastras

Almost everywhere the first Mountain Men, fur trappers and pioneers explored, they found evidence of Spanish mines.

had been located. "The next day we passed a gap in the mountains and came to a place where mining for precious metals had been carried on at some time in the distant past. There were at least 30 old arrastra holes cut in solid rock, each worn from 10" to 14" deep." The march of the Mormon Batallion closely preceded the emigration of the Mormons into the Great Basin, an event which was to signal the discovery of literally hundreds of old Spanish and Indian mines.

In 1847 Brigham Young led his followers into the Great Salt Lake Valley, and within days they began exploring every canyon, desert range and mountain meadow for places to settle and build communities. They searched for timber, coal, iron and lead, all needed to support their new settlements. In only ten years they established 300 towns and cities throughout the Great Basin. They investigated every wilderness place from the peaks of the Sierras to the foothills of the Rockies, and from the Grand Canyon to the Idaho panhandle. Almost everywhere they went they found evidence of ancient mine workings, places where rancherias with cultivated fields had been and ruins of abandoned stone buildings where relics of early Spanish occupation were found. They not only found mines in present day Utah, they also made similar finds at the Salmon River placers in Idaho, the gold outcrops which led to the stampede to Virginia City, Nevada, and the first gold nuggets found at Sutter's Mill in California.

Because the Mormons were a record keeping people, almost every family maintained a daily journal. In those old records are many accounts of old mines found or ruins discovered. But difficult for some to understand today, they did not want to find gold or silver, and it is important to know why they sought only coal to heat their homes, iron for manufacturing and lead for bullets. Brigham Young knew full well that if mines of gold and silver were discovered, it would result in such a stampede of non-Mormons that his people would be overwhelmed. He discouraged his people from seeking precious metals, and criticized those who sought Spanish treasure. Following is a typical statement:

"There is a seal set upon the treasures of the earth, men are allowed to go so far and no further. I know of places where there are treasures in abundance, but can men get them? No! You can read of the treasures of the ancient Nephites, becoming slippery so that when men went to the places where they hid them, they were not there, but were someplace else. Do I run after mines or dig holes in the earth? No, they are like a will-o-the-wisp, a jack-o-lantern!" But Brigham Young's admonition notwithstanding, the Mormons did discover hundreds of old mines in only a few years, although at his order, most of them were never uncovered or worked. And except for some vague reference in some century old journal, they are still lost today. Any modern day treasure hunter would be well advised to research those old Mormon journals.

Probably the first reminder of early Spanish occupation was found only a few miles north of the Salt Lake Valley at the site of Kaysville, where some ruins of a very old stone building were discovered. In a history of Kaysville it is written: "It had generally been thought that the section of Davis County in which Kaysville is located had been uninhabited until the arrival of the pioneers, but white men, whose identity will probably always remain a mystery, lived here much earlier than

1847. Two rude stone structures were found here when the first pioneers arrived. These long abandoned habitations were found on a hillside about two miles south of the townsite." The mystery of the old stone structures was solved several years later by another discovery in nearby Parrish Canyon.

In 1848 Samuel Parrish established a small settlement which in time grew into present Centerville, located several miles south of Kaysville. One of the early settlers there was Thomas Christiansen, who built a grist mill on Parrish Canyon Creek. One day Christiansen with his family climbed high into Parrish Canyon where he found a small cave-like opening. Deciding to explore the cavern, he crawled into the opening, and there before his eyes, covered with the dust of centuries, was an ancient crossbow and pieces of Spanish armor!

To reconstruct why a conquistadore might hide his armor in a mountain cave we need only consider the personal armament each soldier carried. Using the inventory of Coronado's army for comparison, we learn that each officer had three or more sets of heavy castillian armor. Coronado had twelve sets himself! Wearing armor was no doubt very tiring when climbing as steep a mountain as that at Parrish Canyon, so it is easy to see why a weary soldier might cache his armor while he prospected the canyon. There could be any number of reasons why he never returned for it, the possibility that he encountered a band of Indians while not wearing it probably first among them.

The question of why a Spanish explorer had been in Parrish Canyon was answered with the discovery of several old mines there and in adjoining Farmington Canyon. The ore veins had been pretty well worked out by the time they were rediscovered, but several loads of high grade were shipped from what became the Morning Star claims. We can only guess at the connection between the old stone buildings at Kaysville, probably a habitation or a mill site, the cache of armor at Parrish Canyon, perhaps hidden by a weary miner and the old mines in the surrounding canyons, but the puzzle pieces seem to fit together quite well!

Of similar interest is the frequent discovery of

old Spanish coins and artifacts, lost or cached many years ago. When the earliest settlers reached the future site of Parowan in Iron County, one of the first things they did was to dig a hole for a flagpole. "There in the middle of the wilderness, in the protecting arms of the hills at Heap's Springs, where no white man had ever trod," while digging the flagpole hole, Parley Pratt uncovered two Spanish doubloons!

An ancient Jaredite coin from Chief Wakara's treasure cave. Who can solve its riddle? *(Courtesy Utah State Historical Society.)*

A find equally as intriguing occurred where Liberty Park is presently located at Salt Lake City. While digging an irrigation canal, pioneers dug up what they called "an ancient Jaredite coin." Soon afterwards several more of the strange coins were found by settlers exploring for homesteads along the Colorado River near Moab. But the strangest part of the Jaredite coin mystery was yet to be revealed. In 1852 while Ute Chief Wakara was stopped at the cabin of James Martineau at Parowan, Martineau observed some strange coins which Wakara had. Martineau was allowed to examine the coins and noted that they had "hieroglyphics" on them, which he said appeared to be similar to the characters of the Jaredite writings. Martineau saw that several other Indians had some of the same coins, so he asked the chief where they had been obtained. A strange tale unfolded.

Chief Wakara told Martineau that he and his band had taken refuge in a cave along the Escalante River gorge to escape a snow storm, and that in the cave there were countless thousands of the strange coins, spread over its sandy floor. Martineau obtained one of the coins and sent it to Brigham Young, who told him to forget he had ever seen it, and to mention it to no one. The coin found by canal workers at Salt Lake City is now in a private collection; however, numismatist expert Harry Campbell has examined it, and he says it is a British East India Company coin from the mid-1700s. But that doesn't solve the mystery, for we still don't know how the coins came to be buried deep in Salt Lake Valley long before white men settled there, or how a cache of them, no matter whether British or Jaredite, came to be hidden in a remote cave along the Escalante River. As the Mexicans say when confronted with a mystery beyond their comprehension, Quien Sabe?

Some of the first Mormons to search for settlement sites climbed Parley's Canyon and crossed over its 8,000' Golden Pass into Parley's Park and Rhoades Valley. There they came upon an old mine which they later wrote of. "The Mexicans were the earliest miners in Utah, but the extent of their operations will never be known since they filled in their shafts after extracting the ore, or abandoning them for the more profitable trade of slavery. They packed their ores all the way to Santa Fe to be smelted. This fact is evidenced by a remarkable discovery made at Rhoades Valley. A party of prospectors came upon a hole filled with loose dirt, and their curiosity aroused, they excavated it and opened up an old shaft dug many years before by the Mexicans. The hanging wall of the shaft had been cut with iron tools, and a series of steps cut into the wall led down into the shaft, by which steps ore had been carried from the mine. From the bottom of the shaft a tunnel ran for a great distance along the vein. Among the pieces of waste rock were found several good specimens of silver ore."

The writer was undoubtedly mistaken in stating that Mexicans filled in the shaft. Without doubt the shaft was dug under Mexican or Spanish supervision but was filled in by Indians, probably soon after the Ute revolt of 1844, for the dirt in the shaft was still loose when found. Not by coincidence, several other mines were soon located in the mountains above Rhoades Valley, one high on a peak overlooking the Mahogany Hills at the north side of Weber Canyon above present day Hoytsville. When first investigated, the settlers were surprised to find a tunnel secured with a heavy door of wood and iron. They dug the door loose and crawled into the tunnel for 400' before it became too dangerous to proceed further. That is the furtherest the old working has ever been explored, but the Spaniards who placed the door there must have believed something left inside was very valuable to have gone to such effort to secure it. The ancient digging is shown on Froiseth's 1878 map of Utah simple as "Old Spanish Mine."

Another Rhoades Valley mine was found just under a mountain pass below Hoyt Peak. Old Spanish Trail historian Frank Silvey interviewed W.P. Mecham, a pioneer rancher on the Weber River, who recalled that in the fall of the year Mexican pack trains would come from the Hoyt Peak area and camp on his property overnight. The Mexicans unually had about 16 pack mules loaded with bars of bullion which they brought from somewhere in the mountains beyond. The leader of the Mexican miners would pay Mecham for the mules feed in raw gold. Mecham stated that he had no interest in mining and made no effort to back track the mules, something he said he could easily have done. Some years later a prospector named John Young showed Mecham a Spanish map and a journal which was supposed to lead to the mine and tell the history of those who worked there and the amount of gold they dug. Mecham said the journal or waybill appeared to have been written for the use of someone already familiar with the area and its landmarks, but would mean little to anyone not well acquainted with the area. He had no interest in the mine and did not go with Young, but recalled that the waybill read approximately as follows.

"Go into the sierras towards the hill of gold, which you know better than I, to the blue spring. There you will find the place where we washed the ore, the vats and the pans. The mine is on the opposite side of the pass, facing into the morning sun, and is on a direct line with the snowy peak five leagues beyond." Unfortunately neither Mecham or Young had any idea where the "hill of gold" was, or the "blue spring." Young found many springs, but no "vats" or "pans." Apparently Young returned every spring for several years, and one day he chanced upon the old mine. In it he found a small copper chest which contained a silver crucifix and an old parchment document which stated, "You who reach this place, withdraw! This place is dedicated to the Lord, and he who breaks in and steals, on him there shall fall certain death in

this world and eternal condemnation in the next. The gold belongs to God, and not to man!" Young gave little heed to the warning then, but he gave it plenty of thought later on.

Although the ancient tunnel was badly caved, Young reopened it for 50' to where he was stopped by a bulkhead of heavy logs. He was able to reach between the logs and recover several strange looking iron picks, and he could touch what felt like leather bags of ore or something else too heavy to lift. Tons of rocks had settled onto the logs, so he decided to remove the bulkhead with dynamite, but in so doing he caved the entire tunnel in, hopelessly burying the entire diggings. Over the following years Young tried to dig another tunnel into the workings, and when that failed, he attempted to sink a shaft into the tunnel beyond the bulkhead. Time took its toll and Young became an old man before he could sink the shaft through solid rock. A mountain road still leads to John Young's long caved diggings, but they are too dangerous now to enter. The old Spanish tunnel is buried under the waste rock from his diggings, so it looks as if the padre's warning is still true. "The gold belongs to God, and not to man!"

During the 1950s, well known Utah geologist Tom Costas and Joe Peezley discovered an old shaft along the Weber River in sight of Hoyt's Peak and not far from John Young's diggings. Over the shaft stood an ancient pine with a heavy branch growing out over the pit. That branch still has marks worn into it where a rope was pulled across it to raise and lower men and hoist ore sacks from the depths. It is unknown what is hidden in those depths, for a stone dropped can be heard hitting water. Is there a connection between the old shaft by the river and the Spanish mine on Hoyt Peak? As if to leave no doubt about the identity of who worked those old mines in the Kamas hills above Rhoades Valley, in 1858 army troops from General Albert Sidney Johnston's command found an old cannon where it had been left in the long ago. It can still be seen at Salt Lake City, and the date and place where it was cast can be read. Seville, Spain, 1776.

Of all the lost Spanish mines found, the story of the Lincoln Mine is a classic, a lost mine story none can doubt. It was 1858 when Bishop James Rollins with a small party of Mormon explorers

The famous Lincoln Mine, a lost Spanish mine found!

was riding cross country at the southwest end of the Mineral Range in Beaver County, five miles northwest of the future site of Minersville, when they came upon what they later described as "a very old Spanish mine." Even though it had been long abandoned, it was not badly caved, being driven into solid rock. Investigating the inclined shaft more closely, they found that it leveled off into a tunnel where they found rusted pieces of antiquated tools and rotting shoulder yokes used by men to carry heavy buckets of ore from the mine, all of a type never seen before.

Rollins also found a thick vein of ore which he thought was lead, a metal badly needed then, for the Mormons were involved in the Utah War, busily engaged in fighting army troops along the Wyoming border. Brigham Young was advised of their find and quickly authorized the mining of lead for bullets. A crew of men was kept busy at the Rollins Mine, but they had a lot of trouble when they tried to cast bullets from the metal they smelted. When an experienced miner arrived to oversee operations, they soon learned why, for the metal wasn't lead, but nearly pure horn-silver!

In only a few short years a busy mining camp grew up at the edge of the Mineral Range. Other mines were located nearby, including the Rattler, Pioneer and Golden Gate. Ore from the mines was assayed at 3,000 ounces of silver to the ton! In honor of President Lincoln, both the Rollins Mine and the townsite were renamed Lincoln. A smelter was built at nearby Minersville, recovering large quantities of both lead and silver for another fifty years. Even today the old Lincoln Mine, an authentic Spanish mine discovered by Bishop Rollins in 1858, is still being worked on a small scale. To see the old Rollins-Spanish mine for yourself, just follow the Old Spanish Trail westward across the Wasatch Range and trace Father Escalante's tracks south along the Sevier River to the Mineral Mountains. You can't miss it.

CHAPTER EIGHTEEN
SOME FAMOUS LOST MINES

"And the gold of that land is good!"

—Bible, Genesis 2:12

There is no lost mine so well documented or authenticated as the Navajo's Pish-La-Ki, better known to historians as the Lost Merrick & Mitchell Mine. The first Spanish explorers into southern Utah, Pedro de Tovar and Captain Cardenas of Coronado's expedition of 1540, were told of a rich silver mine on the Indian's sacred mountain, somewhere to the west. By 1585 Father Rodriguez had established a mission on the trail leading into that country, followed by Father Romero, who built his mission on the San Juan River in 1628. The old trail that led to Pish-La-Ki passed by both missions.

In his History And Romance Of The Old Spanish Trail, historian Herbert Auerbach wrote, "The Navajos had perfected the art of polishing turquoise and mounting the stones in silver, which they obtained in the form of wire silver from the rocks and melted for their use." The place where the Navajos obtained their wire silver was the fabulous Pish-La-Ki Mine.

Early Spanish miners discovered the Navajo's Pish-La-Ki Mine somewhere on Cerro Negro, what is now Navajo Mountain, on the present Navajo Reservation, west of Oljeto, Utah. They worked it continually until the Indian revolt of 1680, after which it was concealed by the Indians and lost forever to the Spanish. For nearly two centuries the old mine remained unknown except to a few Navajos. In 1863 most of the Navajos were driven from their land by the American army, led by Kit Carson, and were imprisoned at Bosque Redondo, New Mexico. Only old Chief Hoskininni and his small band escaped capture, fleeing into the wilderness of Navajo Mountain.

In 1870, John Merrick, a prospector and adventurer, copied an "old Mexican map" which he found in a California mission, which map showed the location of an old mine on Navajo Mountain which had been worked by Spaniards more than 100 years earlier. Merrick organized a party of California miners, and following the Old Spanish

Trail east and across the San Juan River they located the old mine. Rocks and dirt piled over its entrance had eroded away and the date 1661 could be seen cut into a ledge above its tunnel portal. Merrick and his partners removed a large quantity of silver from the mine and began their long journey back to California. Along the Virgin River they were attacked by Navajos who had followed them, and all were killed except Merrick. He eventually returned to California where he vowed he would never return to Navajo Mountain. Several years later he gave his map to his son Robert, but only on condition that he would not try to find the mine until the country was settled and the Navajos were under control.

In 1879 Robert Merrick arrived at Fort Montezuma on the San Juan River, where he teamed up with Hearndon Mitchell, a son of the Mormon trader there. With several pack animals they crossed Comb Wash and Nokai Mesa heading towards Navajo Mountain. They were never seen alive again, but soon afterwards their bodies were found in Monument Valley, each at the foot of a towering monument about three miles apart, which are still known today as Merrick and Mitchell buttes.

The March 16th, 1880 issue of the *Rocky Mountain News* reported that their bodies had been found by a party of prospectors led by Cass Hite, an old-time miner who spent much of his life searching for the Lost Pish-La-Ki. Empty rifle cartridges strung along the valley floor told of the running fight they had with Indians before being killed and stripped of every possession, including John Merrick's map. Their pack animals were found nearby, as were their pack sacks, still full of nearly pure silver ore! It was commonly believed that Merrick and Mitchell had been killed by Navajos, but in 1939 famed Utah historian Charles Kelly, a life long friend of the Navajos and superintendent of Capitol Reef National Park learned what really happened from Hoskininni Begay, son of old Chief Hoskininni, who had escaped from Kit Carson in 1863.

Hoskininni Begay, last link to the lost silver of Navajo Mountain.

"Finally we came to the south end of Navajo Mountain and came to a little stream with grass. Mother sat on the ground and said she could go no further. Father tried to make her, but she would not, so we made camp there and lived at that place for six years. One day while my father was riding on the mountain he found a place where there was silver in the rocks and brought some home, which he found he could shape without melting. He and six others went back there and brought back more silver, which we made into ornaments. He would never let anyone else see where it came from. In those days all silver was made smooth without design. During the time we lived at Navajo Mountain, our herds increased so that we had plenty of meat and blankets. We also had lots of silver. When we came from the mountains, we were a strong band, and the richest Navajos in the whole country. When we came from the mountains people were surprised to see us. We had never been to a trading post, yet we had much silver, so people said, Chief Hoskininni must have found a silver mine.

Inscription made by Kit Carson, August, 1863, when he drove the Navajos from Navajo Mountain and the Pish-La-Ki Mine. *(Courtesy Utah State Historical Society.)*

"When the whites heard about it, they all came to hunt for the mine. But father would not allow it, so none of the six men who knew about the mine ever told a white man, or even a Navajo, how to find it. I do not even know myself, because when the whites began coming into the country, father would never go there again. When I was about 20 years old, two white men came into our country, found the old mine and took silver from it without being seen. On their way out they passed near our camp. In Monument Valley they were killed by Utes. My father and his people were blamed for killing them, but it is not true. We had nothing to do with it. As you know, when a member of our family dies, their silver is buried with them, so that we no longer have any of the silver from Pish-La-Ki. I myself have had eight wives, and all of my silver is buried with them."

Some years ago a trader on the Navajo Reservation was told by an old Indian how several of the men who recovered Merrick and Mitchell's bodies and their packs of silver ore tried to trace their trail back to the mine, and how everyone of them who tried was killed. Old Chief Hoskininni had instructed an Indian named Tsaynez to kill anyone who ever tried to go to the mine. The trader was also told that many years later a man named Merrick, a descendent of John Merrick, came to the Navajo Mountain country, saying he knew where the mine was and would go to it. The trader warned him not to try, but he went and was killed. The old Navajo told the trader that no white man would ever be allowed to go to the mine of the silver stones. There is no doubt that Pish-La-Ki, the Lost Merrick & Mitchell Mine, exists. The only question is, are you brave enough to search for it?

During the years when the Mormons were exploring their new territory, which at that time included all of the Great Basin from southern California to Wyoming, many old mines were found. In 1857 Joseph Fish wrote, "I have been told by Indians that there is an old gold mine near this place (Fish Lake) which was worked by the Spanish at an early time." Fish continued to explore the Fish Lake country, and one day he and his party came across an old and well worn trail, (The Old Spanish Trail from the Colorado to the Virgin River) which they followed for many miles. Fish wrote that he "found many chunks of lead ore which had been dropped along the trail." Later assays proved the ore to be silver, not lead.

Some years later, Carl Blonquist, a saloon keeper's son from Richfield traded a bottle of whiskey to an Indian friend for several "curiously made gold ingots." The ingots were small and crudely made, as if they had been cast in a sand mold, and were stained with green colored verdigris, indicating they also contained some copper and silver. After several more bottles of whiskey had been exchanged, the Indian agreed to show Blonquist their source. During the dark of night he took Blonquist high onto the Fish Lake Mountain where they entered a narrow slit in the rocks, which opened into a cave. Inside Blonquist saw many ancient looking rotting animal skin bags which had piles of cast ingots and small inch square bars spilling from them. Pieces of rusted armor could also be seen piled against the cavern wall.

He was not allowed to touch anything and was led from the mountain by a strange trail and was told never to try to return to the cave, for the spirits of murdered Indians who had been forced to work in Spanish mines still guarded the treasure there. Every time Blonquist was on the mountain he searched for the cave, but Fish Lake Mountain is a large plateau of weathered and eroded lava rock. There are countless small caves, sinkholes and "blowouts" there. Blonquist never saw the Indian's treasure cave again. With a little luck, you might do better.

A lost mine found and then lost again remains a mystery to this day. The Utah Historical Quarterly for July, 1941 contained the following. "Spanish priests, traders and soldiers of fortune travelled the Old Spanish Trail every year, and there is evidence they prospected for minerals. After the Mormons arrived, they found many old prospect holes in the mountains." One such mine was found by George and Fred Ashdown near the head of Coal Creek Canyon, east of Cedar City. The tunnel was very old and its top caved in, but the two brothers were curious to learn how such an ancient man made place could be found in a land they thought they were the first to explore, so they dug it open and crawled into its depths. The tunnel extended into the mountainside for at least 200 feet, and it still contained many curious looking metal tools. Several made of brass were recovered,

but those made of iron crumbled into pieces as soon as they were picked up.

The Ashdown brothers were not miners, but were looking for a place to establish a sawmill. They took several pieces of shiny black ore from the old mine before continuing their search for a sawmill site. Several months later they gave the pieces of ore to a friend named Ben Evans, and described the place where they had found it. A year passed before Evans had the ore examined at Austin, Nevada, where he learned it was a nearly pure form of hornsilver. Evans hurried back to Cedar City, where he learned the Ashdown brothers had moved on. He never found them again, nor did he ever find their mine on Coal Creek.

The lost Ashdown Mine on Coal Creek might have a connection with a strange event which occurred many years later, during the 1920s. An elderly man of Spanish descent came to Cedar City where he obtained lodging with a local rancher. He had a faded parchment map with him, and after examining it closely he would ride through the Coal Creek country as often as his health would permit. He seemed to be very perplexed that he couldn't find the landmarks he was searching for. Finally, he could ride no more, but before leaving he gave his map to the rancher, telling him that if he could solve its riddle he would locate an old silver mine where his father had worked long ago. He also showed the rancher a small piece of silver ore, which old-timers said was exactly like that found by the Ashdown brothers.

The rancher had little time to waste hunting lost mines, and besides, the old Spanish map appeared to be useless. It had all sorts of strange markings on it, and it showed mountains and valleys he was not familiar with. It appeared to have been torn from a larger map, which if he had might have made the riddle easier to solve. Somewhere in the rugged and colorful cliffs near the head of Coal Creek, there is an old Spanish mine. It will be in very rough country, close to the Cedar Breaks, but if you can find it, it could make you rich!

Indian slavery at the northern mines thrived until the revolt of 1844, but Mexican slavers still made annual trips into Utah Valley even after that time, a practice which would soon be stopped forever. When the Mormons first came to the Great Basin, Indian slavery was a thriving business, engaged in not only by the Mexicans, but even by the Indians themselves. Brigham Young's first order to his followers was to treat the Indians fairly, and even to purchase Indian children if necessary to keep them from being sold as slaves. During the first few years after settlement, several Mexican slaving parties were arrested, and although a few had licenses issued at Santa Fe, they were informed their licenses would not be recognized in Utah Territory. It took several years before the last Mexican slavers came north into Utah, and even longer to stop the Utes from raiding weaker tribes and stealing their children. But in time the Mormon policy of feeding, not fighting the Indians did much to end the practice of slavery. It was Brigham Young's friendship with the Utes, and with Chief Wakara in particular which led to the discovery of what may be the richest and best verified lost gold mine of all time.

The Mormons had travelled a thousand miles through the wilderness to find a home as far removed as possible from anyone else, yet they were hardly settled in the center of the Great Basin before the California gold rush placed them right at the center of the Overland Trail. Almost daily parties of California bound miners arrived at Salt Lake City, anxious to purchase horses or mules and buy fresh supplies of every kind. But they found that commerce at Salt Lake City was strictly a barter affair, for there was no medium of exchange in existence. Some type of money was desperately needed, but the Mormons had no gold or silver to make into coins. In Chief Wakara they found the folution to their problem.

Chief Wakara had already been baptized into the church, and he was anxious to help Brigham Young. When the Mormon leader explained his need for gold, an agreement was made. In July, 1852, Chief Wakara agreed to show someone Young designated as a trusted agent, an Indian mine where there was all the gold he would ever need, but only on the condition that only one man would ever know its location and he would take only enough gold for church use. Chief Wakara wasn't taking any chances of his people ever being forced to work in their own mines again.

As early as 1849 the Mormon church had tried to mint gold coins, but their coin dies were crudely made and their gold supply very limited. According to the ledgers of John Kay, Brigham Young's minter, only $80,000 in gold was minted between 1849 and 1851. After Chief Wakara agreed to furnish all the gold needed, new dies were obtained from England, and after 1852 gold pieces in denominations of $5, $10, and $20 were made in large numbers. The Mormon's money problem was solved and the story of the Lost Rhoades Mine had its birth.

Thomas Rhoades was the man chosen by Brigham Young to bring gold from the Ute's secret mine, and during the next three or four years he brought many pack trains of the precious metal to Salt Lake City, not only enough for the minting of coins but also plenty for other church use. Then Thomas Rhoades became ill and died not long afterwards, but his son, Caleb Rhoades, was allowed to take his father's place and bring gold from the mountains. For many years Caleb Rhoades made many trips to the old Indian mine, and he also had plenty of time to locate other mines nearby, some of which he mined for his own benefit. It is believed that several of them were Spanish mines which had been worked before the Indian revolt of 1844.

For anyone unfamiliar with pioneer Utah, it may seem inconceivable that a group of gold mines could be kept secret for so long a time, but the explanation is simple. The lands where the mines were located was on Indian Reservation land where white men were not allowed, and in such a remote and rugged area that even today it is not well known. Further, both Thomas and Caleb Rhoades took solemn oaths not to reveal the location of the sacred Indian mine, although Caleb Rhoades made no such vow regarding other mines which he discovered himself.

It is quite likely that Pick Murdock, an Indian befriended by Caleb Rhoades, accompanied him to the mines, but there is no record that anyone else ever did. Pick Murdock was the adopted son of Bishop Joseph Murdock, whose son Al Murdock operated the first trading post in Ute country at their village of Whiterocks. On returning from a trip into the mountains with Rhoades, Pick Murdock gave a first-sized chunk of gold to his nephew, Art Murdock, who kept the gold on display at the Whiterocks store for many years. Another large piece of gold was reported by historian Frank Silvey, who talked to an old Indian woman who lived near Moon Lake. She had an egg shaped nugget through which a hole had been drilled so she could wear it on a leather thong around her neck. She told Silvey that the nugget had come from an area just over a ridge from Moon Lake, going towards Rock Creek, where there were many such nuggets only a few inches deep.

The documentation regarding the Rhoades Mine is very detailed, in both church archives as well as in Rhoades' personal journals, but the most believable sources are in United States Congressional files. In 1897 Caleb Rhoades obtained congressional help in having a part of the south slope of the Uinta Mountains removed from Indian reservation status, so that one or more of the mines he had located could be worked. The Indian's sacred mine which he had vowed not to reveal was not included. In exchange he agreed to pay the national debt, which at that time was $250,000,000!

The necessary agreements were signed at Washington, all of which are still available for public scrutiny, with the only delay being the formal opening of the deleted reservation lands for settlement or filing of mining claims. Chief Ouray of the Utes had earlier been to Washington regarding the loss of lands from the reservation, but he could do little to change any agreement made, for none of his people by then knew where any of the old mines were located. In contempt he told the Congressmen, "I and my people came here because we wanted to come. You may give presents to other Indians, but we don't want any presents. You want our land because there is plenty of gold there, but all you are willing to give us for it is copper. Do you think we are fools?" It took several years for the legalities of the lands deletion to become effective, during which time Caleb Rhoades was the only man alive who knew where the mines were located, Chief Wakara and the few Indians who had accompanied Rhoades having long since died. The lands were finally opened to allow filing of mining claims in September, 1905.

Unfortunately the national debt would not be paid, for Caleb Rhoades died on June 2nd, 1905.

There are many clues to the location of the Lost Rhoades Mines. We know they are located on land that was Indian Reservation before 1905. Those lands consist basically of the lower south slopes of the Uinta Mountains, between the Duchesne River and Brush Creek, but most people who have studied Caleb Rhoades' movements generally agree that his mines are in the Moon Lake—Rock Creek area. One or more of the mines are at the base of a cliff in a rock formation not usually associated with gold. Rhoades often said they are in an area where a trained geologist would least likely look, thought by some to mean they are in the foothills rather than high in the mountains. No doubt they are concealed, but they are in an area where there are many Spanish signs. The Moon Lake—Rock Creek area has many old Spanish signs cut into rocks or carved on ancient trees.

Another important point is that it took Rhoades only two weeks to go to the mines from Salt Lake City and return, leading pack animals, which indicates that no time was required to mine the gold, only time enough to load it and return. Because of this many believe he brought back gold from a Spanish cache, possibly from the Lost Jaredite Cache near the old mission on Rock Creek. A clue which suggests that one of the mines might be high on Rock Creek near Stillwater Creek was reported by Frank Silvey. Pieces of ore apparently dropped along a trail have been found there, some assaying as high as $30,000 to the ton. Also, W.P. Mecham, the same rancher that Silvey interviewed regarding the old mines on Hoyt Peak, was crossing from Rock Creek and Stillwater to the Duchesne when he found an old pack sack which still had pieces of ore in it. He had it assayed at Park City and found that it contained five **ounces** of gold and 800 ounces of silver to the ton! For more detailed information on this fabulous treasure, read Footprints In The Wilderness, A History Of The Lost Rhoades Mines, written by Gale Rhoades, a grandson of Caleb Rhoades.

CHAPTER NINETEEN

LOST MINES FOUND

"I cannot say what the truth may be,
I tell the tale that was told to me."

— Walter Scott

In little more than a decade the Mormons explored nearly every valley and range across the Great Basin seeking places to settle. They had colonies from San Bernadino in California to the Lemhi Mission in Idaho, and from the Carson Mission at the foot of the Sierras to Moab on the Colorado. Everywhere they travelled they found the ruins of old mines and missions. They had dug silver from the Lincoln Mine at the edge of the west desert and gold from the Rhoades Mine in the Uintas. It seemed they found old mines everywhere. In 1863 Jacob Hamblin, the famed "Buckskin Prophet," reported "An old mining camp on a well worn trail between Seep Springs and the Grand Canyon, which judging from the packs thrown about looks like a camp where miners were driven away by Indians."

In 1855 William Bringhurst with several others discovered a long deserted mine 25 miles southwest of Las Vegas Springs on the Old Spanish Trail. When he began to reopen the abandoned diggings they found evidence of earlier Spanish mining. Until the end of the Utah War Bringhurst mined lead which was shipped to Salt Lake City by wagon train. In time Bringhurst's find was proven to be the famous Potosi Mine of the Spaniards, mentioned in many old records. Ore from Potosi was rich in silver, but it was located too far from the Mormon settlements to be worked economically. Besides, Brigham Young wasn't interested in silver. It was abandoned after the Utah War when there was no further need for lead.

Other early Spanish diggings were found in the Nevada deserts, as far north as the Oregon border. Long before the coming of the 49ers, Spaniards had already dug for gold at many places in Nevada, at places like Candelaria and Cortez. Silver discoveries at the Comstock Lode made many American millionaires, and one of the newly rich obtained an old Jesuit map, said to have been stolen from the archives at Mexico City. The map

had been drawn during the early 1700s, but still it was very accurate in both latitude and longitude. It showed an old mine north of Boiling Springs, near present Gerlach, another near Ione, one at High Rock Canyon and another in the Pueblo Mountains. Prospectors sent out to search for them failed to locate any, although they did discover old trails in the mountains and several arrastras, proof the mines were nearby. Two of the arrastras, still containing flakes of gold ore, were found in the Shoshoni Mountains above Ione.

One of the arrastras was located at Ione Springs and the other at Spanish Springs. Pieces of ore found at the Spanish Springs site were milled and proven to be rich in gold, but strangely, the quartz rock discovered at the arrastra was of a type of rock not found anywhere nearby. Apparently ore had been packed to the arrastra from some distance, but its source couldn't be located. During the prospector's search they were told by Indians of another old Spanish mine close to Harrison Pass in the Ruby Mountains near Elko, but no more specific location could be obtained.

There are many other references to early mining in Nevada. It is well known that the first American prospectors found Spanish diggings at El Dorado Canyon and Teel's Marsh. Ancient turquoise mines have been found all across southern Nevada, and from the writings of Father Duron in California, we can't help but conclude that they were worked by Spaniards. He wrote, "My Indian servants tell me that on the other side of the Sierras there have long been white men like myself, who speak my language and worship gold." At many ancient basketmaker sites in Nevada, archaeologists have discovered worked turquoise artifacts, as well as polished pendants and beads. At the Lone Mountain Mine in Esmeralda County, fine quality turquoise has been mined from pits 200 feet deep.

Included in other ancient Indian and Spanish

mines is a turquoise mine west of Searchlight, which has been dated to 1300 AD. Still others were discovered by pioneers at Sugar Loaf Mountain and Crescent Peak in Clark County. The Royal Blue Mine at Crow Springs in Esmeralda County reportedly produced more than $5,000,000 after it was rediscovered in 1902. The largest single chunk of turquoise, weighing some 200 pounds, came from Battle Mountain. In the American Archaeologist, M.S. Duffield suggests that "ancient picture writings" in Lincoln County might lead the way to yet another unknown Indian mine.

In a reference book on lost Utah mines one finds, "There are also stories of old Spanish mines in the west desert country, one of them near Marjum Pass in the House Range." There, in that terribly wild and isolated land of bleak windswept peaks, close by the Nevada border, an exciting discovery was made during the 1870s. In North Canyon on the east side of the House Range, an old tunnel entrance was discovered behind a giant boulder. It appeared that the huge rock had been purposedly rolled against the opening, but over the years erosion had loosened it, allowing it to tip away from the entrance. It looked as though Spanish miners may have concealed it themselves, and had intended to return, for inside the tunnel were found several heavy rocks with trigger devices set to cave them onto unwary intruders. Inside the collapsing diggings were found many primitive wooden shoulder yokes for carrying heavy loads, bits of animal skin sacks with metal buckles so fragile they fell to pieces when touched and pieces of unidentifiable metal tools. The traps set for the unwary and the tools may have indicated the owners intended to return.

But even stranger than the traps set in the tunnel were several large sluice boxes made from hollowed logs, found just north of the tunnel canyon. Nothing larger than stunted brush grows anywhere in the House Range, and there isn't enough water to keep a snake alive, much less enough to operate a sluice box. The nearest trees of the size used to build the sluices grow at least 100 miles away, across a dreary desert. The old mine tunnels in North Canyon under the shadow of Sawtooth Peak must have contained extremely valuable ore to warrant bringing such heavy tree trunks from so far away. Who knows what it may have been?

The first settlers at Bluff on the San Juan River were told an enticing tale by Indians they befriended. They learned of a Spanish mine located near the southwest end of the Abajo Mountains. With help of the Indians, several of the pioneers located the long concealed mine. Wind worn signs, names and dates were cut into the sandstone near the mine, but only the date 1760 could be read, all others worn away by the winds of time. The entrance had been covered with rock slid from the mountainside above and the workings were completely caved 40 feet from the surface. The hard pressed pioneers were kept busy wresting a living from the harsh land, so no further work was done and it wasn't long until the mine was lost again.

Indians who lived near Bluff said that in their father's time, Spaniards had packed ore from the mine to somewhere in the south. On their last trip they had left only a few men at the mine, at which time the Indians working there attacked and killed everyone. Those with the slow moving pack train were tracked down and killed also, after which their bodies and even their pack animals and the gold they carried were buried. After Bluff grew into a small town with a general store, old Indians would sometimes trade small pieces of gold for goods. They never denied that the gold came from the place where the miners and their treasure was buried, but no white man was ever clever enough to trick them into telling where the cache was located.

Long before San Juan County was settled, a Mountain Man was hunting for camp meat in the nearby Abajo Mountains when he knocked the front sight from his rifle. At the base of some jagged cliffs he came to a place where there were many small sliver-like pieces of metal rock on the ground. He picked up a piece that was soft enough so that he could force it into the dovetail slot where the sight had been. He was tired and hungry, so he paid little attention to where he found the soft stone. It wasn't until a year or so later when he took his rifle to a gunsmith to have a new sight mounted that he discovered that the soft metal sliver was pure gold!

During the 1880s two prospectors named Dixon and Ducket were hunting for the "Lost Rifle Sight Lode" when they discovered a bonanza vein that assayed 150 ounces of gold to the ton. They located the Gold Queen Mine, built a stamp mill and almost overnight Camp Jackson became the newest mining camp in the San Juan country. Other ledges were located and also produced good ore for several years. But no one ever found the old mine shown to the Bluff pioneers nor did anyone find the Lost Gunsight Lode, and it might be the richest prize of all. It may only be coincidence, but the trail built from Monticello to Camp Jackson passes right by 11,000 foot Abajo Peak to Elk Ridge and the Bear's Ears Pass, the Old Spanish Trail to Navajo Mountain and the Lost Pish-La-Ki Mine!

Several prestigious mining journals began publication during the 1880s, two of the best being the *Mining World Journal of New Mexico* and the *Salt Lake Mining Review.* Both frequently reported the discovery of old Spanish or Jesuit mines. The following are only a fraction of those reported, but they leave little doubt that such mines existed or that many of them had been purposely concealed. "Dr. C.F. Blackington has rediscovered an old mine first discovered in 1655 by Marguerito Luero, one of the followers of Father Guerra, noted priest and missionary. Many shipments of rich ore were made from the mine until 1712, when for some reason it became "lost" and was never heard of again." Today we know that there were several Indian revolts at about the same time it became "lost."

A similar report stated, "An old mine has been found in Tijeras Canyon, with a tunnel 75' into the mountain. Tools of Spanish pattern have been found in it. The oldest Indians living in that area say they have no recollection of mining there, yet the ruins of at least 22 smelters of furnaces have been found, indicating it was a center of enterprising mining ventures. Slag heaps show that silver was the metal mined, and pieces of pure metal can still be found near the ancient furnaces." That could be a good place for someone with a metal detector to check out.

Another article reports, "Mr. F. Manzarares has located several claims believed to be more than 200 years old. His La Plata claim shows a face of silver-galena ore six feet wide. A ruin of an old smelter which had long ago been concealed has also been found nearby, giving indisputable evidence that many mines were operated on a large scale. So intense was the Indian's hatred towards those places in which they had been forced to labor, that they filled in every mine shaft so that no trace of them could ever be found again." During the 200 years from the revolt of 1680 to the 1880s, timbers which had been placed over mine shafts rotted and fell into the depths, opening them to view again, and stones and soil piled over tunnel entrances eroded away or were shaken loose by other natural events.

During the 1870s several ancient mines were uncovered in the Tintic District near Eureka, Utah. A tunnel was found behind a slab or rock which had been slid down over the portal. Behind the stone door miners found a human skeleton and pieces of Spanish armor. I.H. Diehl, a reputable mining engineer investigated. "The methods used by those primitive miners is a marvel. They had no blasting powder or even tools, except those made by themselves, yet they penetrated the solid rock for hundreds of feet. The workings show that fires had been built to heat the face of ore, which was then cracked by throwing water on it." The finder was a lucky man, for the ore in the old tunnel assayed $6,000 to the ton in silver, and it became one of Tintic's best producers.

Mining camp newspapers from Colorado and through Wyoming to Idaho often mentioned miners finding old shafts, arrastras and ruins of old settlements. It is interesting today to see how similar those old accounts are, whether in an Arizona or Utah newspaper or in a New Mexico or Nevada mining journal. A typical report states: "While prospecting with Lopez, a man of Spanish descent, I heard a tale that had been told to him by his father, of an old shaft located in the mountains nearby. Having plenty of time we searched until we found it, in a canyon almost where he said it would be, even though its portal had been purposely walled over with stones. We opened the shaft, one steeply inclined, in which at intervals there were platforms which had served as rest stations for the Indians who hauled the ore out on their backs. We took samples, but they proved to be low grade, containing only a few ounces in gold to the ton, but it did prove to us that Indians did cover up those old shafts to conceal their location."

Still another article stated, "The Indians there

have a tradition of a Spanish mine on a flat top mountain where there are the graves of many Indians. The mountain is red in color and the shaft is covered with a large flat rock." On Utah's Yellowstone River there is such a mountain, with a burial ground atop it. Many people have found pieces of ore on the mountain, but the flat rock covering the shaft has not been found. Some believe that when white men began searching there, Indians covered the flat stone with soil and grass. Sagebrush could be growing above the old shaft now.

In the Cerrillos District of New Mexico there are also many concealed mines, but they are of turquoise, not gold and silver. Some mine tunnels have been located that had closely fitted stones cemented together with mortar across their entries. "In an old mine reopened near Cerrillos there is a vein of turquoise 2" wide, and inside the deep workings a quartz vein rich in gold has been found. The mine is as safe to enter as the day it was dug more than 200 years ago, being driven into solid rock." In 1880 at the Eureka District of New Mexico, "Mr. D.C. Hyde found a number of sealed up caves in which there are good veins of turquoise, as well as a gold bearing vein on a wall in the central cave. Investigators believe that turquoise has been mined there for 1,200 years." Another find was made in the Gallinas Mountains where "Wire gold in quartz has been discovered in a shaft worked hundreds of years ago. Even the slag pile found near the mine has yielded a high gold content."

Not every old mine found was an El Dorado, for many were shallow and soon worked out. It was a common saying among old-time miners that at Spanish mines where work had not been interrupted by Indian troubles, a man could expect to find very little ore left. There were also mines with high grade ore, but which couldn't be sunk deep into the ground because of heavy water flows. At many mines not enough high grade ore or bullion could be produced by the methods then used to warrant packing the ore all the way to Santa Fe. Frequently high grade or bullion bars from a number of small mines was cached together at some central place until a sufficient amount had been accumulated to make a pack train worth while. In 1888 a man named Hershcell Hill found

just such a place.

It is said that Hill was a trained mining engineer, and that he was searching the bleak Sevier Desert country of west central Utah for an old mine he had acquired a map to. This is the same region that Father Rivera explored in 1761, and where his guides, the Munez brothers prospected and mined several years later. Hill made several trips into the desolate and waterless country between Pavant Butte and the San Francisco Mountains without success. Late in the year with winter storms fast approaching he made one last trip into the black volcanic rock desert, where he became hopelessly lost in a blinding snowstorm.

Hill was wandering through the storm trying to find some kind of shelter when he came to a low-lying rocky ledge of rock. He felt his way along the ledge until he came to a narrow slit-like opening. Hill crawled into a small chamber out of the storm, and in the darkness quickly fell into an exhausted sleep. When he awakened he found himself in a small cavern, nearly filled with rotted leather pack-sacks. From their dried and split sides little streams of gold nuggets and pieces of gold laced quartz had spilled onto the cavern floor. Hill recognized that there was a king's ransom in front of him, but he also knew that he was lost in a desert almost without landmarks. Filling his pockets, he began the long hike eastward to where he knew the little town of Fillmore was located. He tried to keep track of his trail, but when he looked back he was surprised to see how the low line of gray rock blended into the desert sand.

Hill reached Fillmore sometime the next day, delirious from three days without water. Friends at Fillmore later told him that the place he described sounded like the Crickett Hills, a low range of rocky outcrops sometimes standing a few feet above the desert dunes and sometimes buried by them. It took Hill a week to recuperate, but after selling the gold he had taken from the cavern for $3,000, he outfitted to return to the desert cache. The winds of winter blew sandstorms as dark as night at mid-day, and although he made trip after trip into the desert, he never saw the rocky outcrops again. He could see Pavant Butte far to the north and Frisco Peak to the south, just as he had seen when he became lost in the storm and found the treasure cave, but the Crickett Hills were nowhere to be found. Those who know the Sevier Desert still wait for another storm to uncover the rocky outcrop where a narrow opening leads into a cavern filled with bags of gold. It has been a long wait.

CHAPTER TWENTY
THE LOST JOSEPHINE DE MARTINIQUE

"Ignore the hoard of gold once hid,
Make no attempt to lay your hand
On what the Gods have held taboo!"

—Horace

There has been no lost mine more sought after than the fabulous Josephine de Martinique. Nor is there one with more historical evidence to support its authenticity. References to it can be found in both church and civil archives as well as in records of the King's Quinto paid on gold shipments made from it. The Bear's Ears section of the Old Spanish Trail had no other purpose than to serve the Josephine Mine. From the earliest explorers and adventurers such as Father Posada during the 1630s to miner-historians like Edgar Wolverton who traced its route in the 1920s, all knew the old trail led only to the Josephine.

Countless others whose names will probably always remain unknown followed the old trail from Monument Valley to the San Juan River and the Bear's Ears Pass in the Abajos. They crossed the Colorado near the head of Cataract Canyon at Spanish Bottoms and trekked westward to the Standing Up Country and beyond Sunset Pass to Lands End, and continued west to the Burr Desert and the Henry Mountains. In the Henrys there are giant pines growing among the ruins of centuries old smelters and arrastra sites. They have been tree ring dated back to the mid-1600s.

One of the first "modern" accounts of discovery along the Bear's Ears Trail can be found in the journals of John C. Fremont's fifth expedition of 1853. He was one of the first American explorers to note the stone steps cut into the canyon walls above Spanish Bottoms, chiseled into the sandstone cliffs so mules could climb out of the near vertical canyon. He also noted the old trail worn deep into the sandstone desert, made by countless pack trains in the distant past. It was along that worn trail that he made an exciting discovery. His notes describe finding "the very old bones of pack mules, and on either side of them scattered piles of gold ore from packsacks long since weathered away."

Traces of the Old Spanish Trail, steps cut into stone and the trail worn deep into the sandstone desert, can still be found in Utah's canyonlands country.

In January, 1854, Fremont's party was caught in a raging mountain blizzard. They were forced to make a desperate march to the Mormon outpost at Parowan, where several of his men were treated for frostbite and badly frozen limbs. Still, they were greatly excited over the gold they had found along the trail. Several years later, one of those who had been treated at Parowan returned with a prospecting outfit, making it no secret that he was going to follow the old trail to his fortune. He started out bravely enough, but returned a few weeks later, wild-eyed and exhausted, with all of his fine outfit missing. He told how he came to a canyon impossible to cross, where Indians stole everything from him, even his rifle and food. He never returned to Parowan, but he may have been the man known as Burke who tried again several years later.

In 1868 a man who called himself John Burke rode into Ben Bowen's stage station at Desert Springs, telling a tale that he alone knew where the lost Spanish mine of the Henry Mountains was hidden. Bowen was anxious to go with Burke, so taking a third man named Blackburn along as a camp tender and wrangler, they followed Fremont's trail of 1853. They purchased a few last supplies from a rancher at Blue Valley, where they were warned against going into the Henrys. The rancher told them that several years before an Indian had worked for him, and one day as they rode in the mountains near Mt. Ellen the Indian said, "There is plenty gold up there!"

When questioned, the Indian told the rancher of an old Spanish mine where his grandfathers had been forced to work. They were branded with hot irons and punished terribly for trying to escape. One day the Indians revolted, and although many of them died, they drove the Spaniards from the mountains and hid every sign of the hated mines. Their medicine man then placed a curse on the mine, "That to him who reopens the mine will come great calamity. His blood will turn to water, and even in his youth he will be as an old man. His squaws and papooses will die, and the earth will bring forth for him only poison weeds instead of corn!"

The rancher warned that Indians still guarded the old workings, and that only bad luck would come from seeking them. But the three prospectors scoffed at his warning and continued on, entering the mountains around the north side of Mt. Ellen, where they crossed the headwaters of Cresent Creek and made camp. Burke and Bowen climbed to a place already known to Burke, an outcropping ledge of gold ore in which a shaft had been sunk many years before. There was no way to climb down the dangerous shaft, but they were able to break enough gold laced quartz from the ledge to fill their pack sacks.

To save time they left the mountains through Penn-Ellen Pass, heading towards the little Mormon hamlet of Pleasant Dale, 50 miles across an unknown desert to the northwest. From the 11,000 foot Henrys, the desert below them appeared to be flat, but when they began to cross it they discovered a maze of deep canyons and broken cliffs. Suffering from thirst, Burke and Bowen ignored Blackburn's warning and drank from a stagnant pool. Both were deathly ill by the time they reached Pleasant Dale. After recuperating a few days they went to Salt Lake City where they sold their gold for $1,500.

On their way back to Desert Springs, Bowen became violently ill and died while crossing Rabbit Valley. Only a few days after reaching Desert Springs Burke died also. Was it because they drank poisoned water, or was it the Indian curse? Although Blackburn had not been to the mine site himself, he knew approximately where it was from where they had camped and cached their tools under an ancient pine. Blackburn thought he would have no trouble finding the mine, but although he made several trips into the mountains and did locate the camp site and tool cache, he could not follow the trail beyond. He often saw Indians following him, and later said they had covered the old shaft so he couldn't find it. Every time he went into the Henrys, something had happened to him, either sickness, his camp supplies stolen or his horses stampeded. Twice he returned home to find a family member dead. Believing the Indian curse had followed him, he gave up searching, saying, "Because of that mine sickness and bad luck followed me and my family for 30 years!"

For a dozen years more the ancient Josephine Mine was not disturbed, but in 1885 a gold strike was made on the placers along Cresent Creek, and a rush of miners hurried to the mountains. A rough camp named Eagle City exploded near the head of Cresent Creek. Summers & Butler, operators of the Bromide mine, built a stamp mill, as did Kimball & Turner at their Oro Mine. Both were hard rock mines, not placers. Meanwhile a mining journal reported an exciting find made in the next canyon south. "A large glob of gold has been found along Copper Creek in the Henry Mountains. An assayer has verified that it had been melted in some type of a midden (a cast iron pot), probably very long ago judging from the weathered markings on it."

Jack Moore, later a "long rider" with the Wild Bunch, ran a saloon at Eagle City, and occasionally an Indian would bring gray colored rocks

Every time it rains the old shaft is exposed. The lost Josephine de Martinique Mine.

heavily encrusted with wire gold to his saloon, which he would trade for whiskey. He was very secretive and only appeared when Moore was alone. Once he told the saloon keeper that the gold came from a ledge by the side of an old shaft, where "every time it rains the gold is exposed." No doubt he lost no time covering the ledge after every storm, for no one ever found it.

Two men who knew the Henrys better than most were Charley Hanks and Frank Lawler. Hanks carried the mail from Green River to Eagle City and spent a lot of time prospecting the mountains, while Lawler was one of the original miners there. Known as the Hermit of The Henrys, he lived alone at the ghost of Eagle City from 1911 until his recent death. Hanks discovered an ancient ore crushing site, a square trough cut into solid rock, where ore had been crushed by dragging a heavy square stone back and forth. Pieces of ore picked up near the crude mill assayed $5,000 to the ton in gold! The dim outline of a trail led into the mountains from the primitive mill, and along it strange signs and dates had been cut into the ledge rock, but the trail was lost where great rock slides had covered it in the long ago.

Frank Lawwler made an even more exciting discovery at his placers on Cresent Creek. At one place he dug a pit 35' deep to bedrock, where unbelievably he uncovered the portal of an ancient

tunnel! The very fact that it was covered so deeply with sand and gravel indicated its antiquity. It had been timbered with tree trunks, but Lawler couldn't find a single stump on the mountains nearby. He determined that the trees had been cut so long before that their stumps had rotted completely away. Within only a few days his diggings began to fill with water from the old tunnel and caved in. The old man was never able to reopen it again.

It wasn't until the arrival of Edgar T. Wolverton at the turn of the century that the Henrys began to reveal their secrets. In 1900, Wolverton, a trained engineer, began searching for the Burke & Bowen diggings, which he was certain was the famous Lost Josephine. Living alone for more than 20 years, he explored every gulch and ridge across the mountains, and he made many startling discoveries. He found old smelter sites and piles of slag so old that pine trees with more than 100 annual rings were growing on them. He dug into one old pit he estimated to be 175 years old and found pieces of melted gold and the remains of a stone furnace.

Wolverton kept a daily journal which contains fascinating descriptions of his explorations and amazing finds. Some were typical of the man killing work he did all by himself. "Location work done, camp put up, trail opened, mill built. Problems make any work except the most necessary very difficult." With only a few words, such as "mill built," he described back breaking labor which took months or even years to complete.

By the 1920s Wolverton had located what may have been the Lost Josephine. His journal entry of July 21st, 1921, reads, "Found the old Mexican

200 years after the revolt of 1680 Wolverton found the ruins of Spanish arrastras.

mill today while panning on the hill south of camp. Sack of ore brought down. . . . (illegible) . . . , a very hard day, tired and thirsty. . . ." That was his last entry, for the next day his horse fell and threw him across the saddle horn, breaking his bladder in a very painful injury. He was found several days later by a sheep herder who took him to a hospital at Fruita, Colorado, where after an emergency operation he died. Edgar T. Wolverton is buried at the now ghost town cemetery at Elgin. Appropriately, his tombstone is a drag stone from a Spanish arrastra he found in the Henrys. With Wolverton died the secret of the Lost Josephine.

One could get the impression that lost Spanish mines are never found, forgetting of course the many which are, such as the Lincoln Mine. One might even believe that stories of concealed Jesuit mines are exaggerated, that is if he wasn't aware of the Old spanish Mines Mining Company. In 1893 Robert M. Keen was operating a hotel at the Baldy Mining Camp in New Mexico. There he met Joe Guiterez, who told him that when he was only eight years old his father and some other miners were killed by Indians near where they were working an old Spanish mine in central Utah. Guiterez had been with his father and was one of the few who had escaped the massacre, and none of them ever returned to the mine.

Keen was fascinated by the story, and he finally convinced Guiterez to help him find the mine. It took them several years to save enough money to buy a prospecting outfit and another year to locate the landmarks Guiterez still remembered. Guiterez could recall several large black volcanic cones and a creek where Indians grew corn near a large village. They followed the Old Spanish Trail past Fish Lake to the Sevier River, which they followed to Clear Creek Canyon. There they turned north into the desert country where they found the black volcanic cones, 14 miles south of Fillmore. There was the Indian village of Kanosh and Corn Creek flowing out of the Pavant Range. The pieces all fit together.

Near the head of Corn Creek they discovered several unusual looking sunken depressions in the ground, which they dug into. They proved to be two very old shafts which had been concealed by placing heavy logs across them. Over the years grass and wild flowers had begun growing on top of the logs. With great care the shafts were uncovered, and a hand cranked windlass hoist was built over one of them. Two men were hired to help with the work, and it was only a few days before Keen was lowered into the shaft, where he found it to be 140 feet deep with four side drifts or levels in its depths. At each level a large flat stone had been placed into a groove chiseled into the solid rock. Rotted sections of notched log chicken ladders were found still braced against the stone landings.

The shafts were judged to be too dangerous to reopen, so a stock company was organized, appropriately named The Old Spanish Mines Mining Company, with Keen as General Manager. With a crew of miners, a tunnel was driven from lower on the mountain to connect with the shaft bottom. While driving the tunnel, a body of telluride ore with gold values of $1,400 to the ton was found. In the words of Manager Keen as reported in the Salt Lake Mining Journal, "This begins to look encouraging!" So if you don't believe that old Spanish mines are ever found, just follow the progress of the Old Spanish Mines Company in the Salt Lake Mining Review, beginning in February, 1901. That ought to convince you!

Another Spanish mine found was the Josephine Mine on Currant Creek in Utah's Wasatch County, not to be confused with the Josephine de Martinique of the Henry Mountains. Currant Creek was on the Dominguez-Escalante trail, which they noted crossing on September 20th, 1776. The fathers did not venture up Currant Creek, but instead continued west past Strawberry Valley to Utah Lake, so we do not know whether or not the old mines were being worked at that time. We do know that not long after the settlement of Heber Valley in 1859 two old mines were discovered. An early issue of the Wasatch Wave reported "the discovery of the Lost Josephine Mine near a mountain lake where an ancient arrastra has also been found."

Apparently the settlers were too busy farming to engage in mining at that time, but their interests were certainly revived a few years later when the Wave reported, "An old mine uncovered on Currant Creek is believed to be the Lost Josephine. Ancient tools have been found and ore values are reported to be sensational!" At about that same time prospectors discovered gold placers on Currant Creek at "the narrows," just below the two old mines. While investigating the placers, miners discovered an ancient stone diversion dam on the creek and the remains of several old sluice boxes made from hollowed logs.

George Olson was one of the miners sent by Heber City businessmen to reopen the old mine, actually two separate tunnels close together, driven into the mountain at different angles. It was a difficult and dangerous job, and Olson's crew of miners had retimbered only one tunnel for 125' when the promoters ran out of money. One of the businessmen devised a scheme to get stockholders to finance further work. With a shotgun, he highgraded the diggings by firing several loads of fine gold into the caved rock where the miners were working. When he brought several of Olson's friends to the mine to see the rich ore they had struck, Olson exposed the fraud rather than let his friends be swindled, and with no funds to pay the miners, work stopped.

Over the years the tunnel reopened by Olson has caved in again, but the chance is still there if you're interested. If you'd like to see what's at the end of the tunnel, just follow Currant Creek upstream twelve miles from where it crosses US-40. You will have to hike about three miles up a ridge to the right above "the narrows," to the base of a broken red ledge. Rotted logs show where Olson's cabin stood and second growth aspen trees nearly cover the old mine dump. Olson and his miners never learned what was at the tunnels end, but whatever it is, it's still there!

CHAPTER TWENTY-ONE

SOME LEGENDS COME TRUE

"Gold is where you find it."

—Old Miner's Proverb

El Mina del Tiro, the mine of the shaft, added as much gold and silver to the king's treasury as any Spanish mine. It was "a very old Indian mine" when first discovered by Espejo in 1580. Under Spanish supervision it was worked for 100 years, until the Indian revolt of 1680. By the time the Spaniards returned to the northern mountains every trace of it had disappeared, but a find made two centuries later may have solved the riddle of its strange disappearance. The discovery was made not far south of Westcliff in Huerfano County, Colorado, where one can look across the 14,000' peaks of the Sangre de Cristo (Blood of Christ) Mountains.

It is a land of legends and lost Spanish mines, including LaCaverna de Oro, the cave of gold. The cavern may be the long lost El Mina del Tiro. The cavern was discovered by Elija Horn in 1869. An early resident of that area, Horn was exploring what are known locally as the Crestone Needles, when he came upon a Maltese Cross cut into a ledge high on the mountain, by the side of a narrow

The gold is at the bottom of the shaft at El Mina de Tiro.

slit-like opening. The opening had been covered with rocks in the distant past, but the whims of nature had loosened them enough to reveal an entranceway.

Horn was unable to descend the near vertical shaft inside, but he did explore a short side drift where he made a gruesome discovery, a skeleton in Spanish armor! Several arrowheads still lodged in the bones told the cause of death. Apparently Horn made no further attempt to investigate the shaft, and it wasn't until 1891 that a party from Denver led by Don De Foe explored a cave in the Crestone Needles, where they found four skeletons. Because there are a number of caves in the needles, it isn't known for sure that the cavern explored by De Foe was the same one found by Horn.

In 1919 an old Mexican woman, then said to be 105 years old and who lived five years longer, told a tale of a fabulous Spanish gold mine hidden deep in the mountains near the Crestone Needles. She told how her ancestors had been worked as slaves there in the long ago, and also how her people had risen up and drove the Spaniards from the mountains. The huge pile of gold the Spaniards were forced to leave when they fled was thrown into a shaft where priests had cut a cross into a rock ledge. All of their tools and ladders were dropped into the shaft and slide rock was pushed into it. There wasn't enough rock to fill the shaft, for it had been driven so high on the mountain that the waste rock made a long rockslide into the canyon below.

A party was organized to search for the place the old woman had described and as she had told, a portal was found, and by its side a faded Maltese Cross. The sides of the shaft were loose and dangerous, so that work had to progress slowly. Seventy feet below the opening a short side drift was found, and in it a crude log ladder which was later judged to be 200 years old. At 90 feet in depth the narrow pit opened into a 20 foot circular shaft.

In another side drift 300 feet below the collar of the shaft, an ancient hand forged hammer of seventeenth century design was found. The searchers were able to descend 500 feet before they encountered the loose rock which had been dumped into the shaft. The walls had giant slabs of rock so loose they could fall at the slightest touch, which prevented further exploration.

Records do not reveal any further exploration of the old shaft until 1932 when a party led by Peter Moser made a very thorough and painstaking investigation. With better equipment and lighting they discovered a nearly hidden side tunnel 400 feet below the surface. Carefully removing caved rock they inched their way forward for 50', where they made a grisly discovery. At the end of the tunnel they found a human skeleton chained by the neck to an iron ring set in the stone wall!

Also of interest is something else the old Mexican woman said. She recalled that much lower on the mountain a tunnel connected with the shaft bottom. A heavy wooden door which had been torn from the miner's mission had been placed over the tunnel entrance and then covered with large stones. Searchers climbed the sharp crags and loose slide rock, and about 1,000' below the shaft entrance they found the ruins of an old stone building, thought by some to be the mine mission. But search failed to locate the wooden door and tunnel entrance which would lead to the gold at the bottom of the shaft. Many believe that the old Mexican woman's Caverna de Oro and El Mina del Tiro are one and the same. Only time will tell.

An equally exciting discovery was made on Recapture Creek, a small desert stream which flows into the San Juan River near Old Fort Montezuma in San Juan County, Utah. When the first pioneers arrived at Fort Montezuma they found an old hermit already living there. It took some time to make friends with him, but in time he told them a tale that when the Emperor Montezuma's servant fled north to hide the royal treasure, he was recaptured at the little creek he called Recapture Creek, by which name it is still known today. It's doubtful that the settlers believed his story, but they had to believe the gold the hermit had, for in time they saw plenty of it. Whenever the old man needed supplies he would appear at either Bluff or the fort's trading post,

where with a hand axe he would cut enough gold from a small bar to pay his bill. The bars were about an inch square and six to eight inches long. Those who saw them or the pieces he used to pay the trader with remembered that there were Spanish numerals or letters on them.

The mystery of the hermit's gold excited attention again in 1905 when Andy Laney, a cowboy working for the Scorup Ranch near Monticello, stopped to water his horse on Recapture Creek. Laney saw something shining through the water, and investigating, he dug a bar of gold from the sand. It was about 8 inches long and crudely cast, and had words and numbers which were strange to him, as well as a Catholic cross which he recognized. Laney lost no time selling the bar when he was offered $1,800 for it, more money then he thought existed. But the money was soon spent at the Blue Goose Saloon at Monticello or at other dives.

With a partner named Blaine, Laney returned to Recapture Creek. For weeks they searched for another bar without luck, and then one day when they were about to give up, quite by accident Blaine stepped on a bar barely covered by sand about 100 feet from the creek. Digging furiously they soon uncovered four more bars, as well as a chunk of gold about the size of a clenched fist. They quickly went to their favorite saloon at Dolores, Colorado, where Blaine was killed while allegedly cheating at cards. Laney returned to cowboying when his money was gone. It was later reported that he was killed somewhere near Navajo Mountain by some of Chief Posey's outlaws.

That would have closed the mystery of the gold bars if two hunters looking for relics along Recapture Creek hadn't found two more gold bars in 1964. And a newspaper reported in 1979 how a man and his wife had camped overnight on Recapture Creek, and while using metal detectors to search for coins, found still another bar. No one can say for sure where they come from. Some believe the hermit's tale of Montezuma's treasure is true, but a more likely explanation might be that like the mule skeletons and gold ore found by Fremont, the gold bars of Recapture Creek are part of a Spanish gold shipment being packed from the Lost Josephine Mine to some gulf port. We do know one thing for sure, Recapture Creek is right on the Old Spanish Trail!

You may not believe that Montezuma's Aztecs hid the emperor's treasure anywhere near Recapture Creek, but a lot of people at the little town of Kanab, just north of the Arizona line, think it was hidden not far from where they live. When Cortez fought his way into Mexico City for the second time, he discovered that most of Montezuma's treasure was gone. He learned that his servant had taken it far to the north to their ancestral home where it was cached in a secret cave. Although to some it may sound strange, many people at Kanab believe that some sort of Indian treasure is buried just north of their town.

The tale of Montezuma's treasure cave had its origin in the writings of Cortez's chronicler, who recorded, "The Emperor's servant Tlahuicle took many loads of gold and jewels so far to the north that no one could ever find it." In 1920 a character named Freddie Crystal arrived at Kanab and started asking questions about the mountains near town. He had an ancient looking map in his possession, which he said would lead the way to Montezuma's treasure. The map showed a place where petroglyphs would lead the way to a canyon having four forks, surrounded by four peaks, one at each point of the compass. In the center of the quadrant formed by the four peaks there would be a lone mountain, where the treasure was hidden in a cave. Old-timers familiar with the area studied Crystal's map and saw that it matched the exact topography of Johnson Canyon and the White Mountain!

With everyone anxious to help find the treasure, Kanab became a deserted village, with every able-bodied person hurrying to the new tent town erected at the edge of White Mountain. Just as the map directed, petroglyphs and ancient hand cut stone steps were found leading up the mountain side. They led to a place where the mouth of a tunnel was walled over with squared blocks of stone cemented together with mortar. To add to the mystery, the stones were of granite rock not found in that area, while the mortar proved to be made of a fine gypsum sand mixed with animal blood. The nearest sand of that type was found only at White Sands, New Mexico!

When the wall was dug away, a tunnel 14 feet square was exposed, but 60' into the tunnel a second stone and mortar wall exactly like the first was encountered. With considerable effort it too was dug away, but 160 feet into the mountain a third stone wall was found. By then all but the most zealous workers had returned to their homes, but Freddie Crystal and a small but dedicated crew continued working. When the third wall was removed, a large chamber with a cement like floor was found, with a maze of tunnels leading from it, each closed off by a solid stone wall. It appeared that White Mountain was honeycombed with tunnels and chambers. To discourage the faint-hearted, deadly traps were encountered, huge delicately balanced boulders triggered when pieces of the stone walls were removed.

The excavation of the mysterious White Mountain had already taken more than two years, with no end of its puzzling underground maze of tunnels in sight. Many who had helped with the digging ran out of money and had to return to their farms or ranches. With no one left to help him, Freddie Crystal left as quietly as he had arrived. If you're a treasure hunter, you can't fail to see the similarity between the White Mountain diggings and the mysterious money pit at Oak Island. Were they both built for the same purpose, and if so, by who? For anyone interested in becoming rich, White Mountain and its Aztec treasure cave is still there. Almost anyone at Kanab can point the way to Montezuma's treasure cave.

Not long after Mormon pioneers settled Utah Valley, they began building settlements at the same places where Fathers Salmeron, Posada and Escalante had camped before them. During their first years in the valley it was a common sight to see Mexican slavers pass through the valley going toward the northwest during the spring of the year and see pack trains loaded with gold and silver ore come down the canyons from the south and east in the fall of the year. Journals of many early settlers describe such slaving or mining parties. One account of 1852 written by Mormon V. Selman is of particular interest. He described how Spanish (Mexican) pack trains carrying gold ore would come down the Provo River Canyon and camp overnight near his little farm. "They would camp by our place for a few days to rest their pack animals. Those mules were loaded with packs which did not look very large, but they were all they could carry. They kept an armed guard at their camp and no one was allowed near, as if whatever was in those packs was very valuable."

As stated earlier, one of the first actions taken by Brigham Young was to prohibit slavery. In 1852, the same year Selman reported the gold miners camped at his place, Marshal William H. Kimball arrested a party of Mexicans as they were leaving Utah Valley through Spanish Fork Canyon. The slavers reluctantly surrendered the Indian children they had captured, telling the marshal that slaving was the most lucrative business they had engaged in since packing gold ore from the mountains. When questioned further, the slavers told how they had packed gold from the Mine Of The Yutahs in the mountains above Utah Valley, and from other mines on the Provo and Weber rivers, as well as from the Uinta Mountains. Within only a few years after Brigham Young's ban on slavery and with farms closing the old trails, Mexican slavers and ore pack trains were seldom seen. But occasionally a small party or a lone individual would return to the mountains, tempted with the knowledge of certain wealth to be found there. One who returned had been a small boy with the miners who camped at Selman's farm in 1852.

In 1921 an aged Mexican said to be 80 years old came to Provo City where he found employment with a contractor who was building city sidewalks. He proved to be a good worker, but when he received his pay he quit his job and wasn't seen again for several months. Then he came back to his former employer and asked to be rehired. Because he had been a hard worker, he was given his old job, but only to quit when payday came again. A month later he returned once more, but the contractor told him he could not be rehired if he intended to quit again. The old man said that he needed the money badly, for he had travelled a long ways and needed supplies so he could continue his search for an old mine where he had had been with his father long ago. He said that on their last trip to the mine they had taken all of the bullion their mules could carry, but still they had to leave a cache of silver bars behind. They had intended to return, but Indians attacked and killed several of the party not far south of Spanish Fork Canyon, and with the Mormon ban on Mexicans and with settlements at every spring and water hole, they

had been afraid to return.

The contractor recognized the similarity of the old man's story and a record which he had read which had been written by Daniel Jones of the Mormon Batallion. Jones, in writing about the annual Mexican pack trains which took gold to Santa Fe told a fascinating tale of "the descendents of Coronado," Mexicans at Santa Fe, who secretly worked mines near Utah Lake and packed their gold and silver south without obtaining a permit to do so, or paying taxes on it. "They went into the north where they worked at mining, keeping silent about it and keeping the gold for themselves, without paying the required tax. Some even took wives among the Indians, and all went well until they had accumulated several million dollars. They started south with their treasure, but the Indians they had treated shamefully at their mines followed, attacking and killing their former masters. They then buried all of the gold. When the annual pack train did not arrive at Santa Fe, their children went north and found the place of massacre, but they could not find the place where the gold was buried."

Quite reluctantly the old man admitted that he had a map which should lead him to the mine; however, he could not find the needed landmarks. The contractor said that he was well acquainted with all of the canyons and mountains nearby, and that if he could look at the map he might be able to help him. The Mexican hesitantly unrolled a piece of goatskin on which the map was drawn, but then changing his mind quickly rerolled it, but not before the contractor got a good look at it. The map was so simple he easily recognized its landmarks. He asked the old man where he had been searching, and when he waved his hand towards Spanish Fork Canyon, the contractor told him he had been looking in the wrong place. Instantly the old man became very angry, saying that he knew more about the mine's location than anyone else, for he had once been there himself. Refusing his employer's help, he stalked away and was never seen around Provo again.

The landmarks on the Mexican's map were very few and easily recognized by anyone familiar with the area. It showed Utah Lake and a river flowing into it. At the river's first fork a valley was shown, beyond which the stream divided and forked again below two twin peaks. The mine was marked on the left fork below the peaks, where several graves were marked on a ridge. When his job was completed, it took the contractor only a few trips into the mountains before he found the stream forks and the twin peaks, and below them he found a cave-like opening where the ridge dropped sharply to the valley below. The old workings were badly caved, but with help he removed fallen rock from the tunnel and retimbered it with aspen tree trunks.

It soon became obvious that the cavern had been occupied by man over a long period of time, for many animal bones, including several buffalo skulls were uncovered, as well as places where cooking fires had been. The skulls indicated how old the workings were, for buffalo were gone from those valleys before the first Mormons arrived, although early trappers mentioned finding their bones during the early 1800s. Little mineralized rock was found, and no cache of bullion bars, but something very intriguing was dug from the old tunnel. While removing caved rock several old Spanish tools were uncovered, as well as a flat piece of highly polished animal bone, approximately the size of a man's hand. On it was inscribed an exact copy of the map owned by the old Mexican!

The old bone map was exactly and carefully made, correct in its every detail. In addition to the map of Utah Lake and the river with its forks and the twin peaks, it also had a series of lines which later proved to be an exact outline of the tunnels and shafts found in the cavern. It had the outline of nearby mountains inscribed around its edge, and four holes drilled through the bone exactly matched the locations of several other known Spanish mines, including the Josephine Mine on Currant Creek and the Boren and Bethers Mine in Daniels Canyon. The bone map was especially well made, as carefully inscribed as could be done in a modern machine shop, yet it had been found under tons of rock in a cavern where Spanish miners worked in ancient times.

In 1896 Bill Bethers, a Heber City pioneer discovered what he called "hieroglyphics" on a rock in Daniels Canyon, just one canyon northeast of the cavern thought to be the Lost Mine Of The Yutahs. Bill Bethers brought a man "accustomed to reading such signs" to the canyon, where he interpreted them as "representing a figure of a man with his hands thrown up as if suddenly surprised, another as a burro or pack animal, and others perfectly visible but undecipherable." The entire "hieroglyph" was determined to be a guide for miners returning to the canyon after a long absence.

Bethers, with his neighbor Henry Boren, explored the side canyons and ridges near the "hieroglyph" until they found a long abandoned mine working which consisted of two tunnels driven into solid rock, their portals covered with loose rock as though purposely concealed. One of the tunnels was reopened for 75 feet before winter came. Both Boren and Bethers intended to return to the mine in the spring, but the necessity of working their farms took all of their time. Before long both men were called to settle other areas, so the old mine was never explored further.

But the real mystery is how that old bone map, an exact copy of the Mexican's map which we know was ancient, came to be lost, or hidden, under tons of fallen rock in an old mine high above Utah Valley. Whether the cavern is really the Lost Mine of The Yutahs is still unknown, for a lot of work remains to be done before whatever lies beyond its caved workings is known. Hopefully its secret will soon be revealed. But in the meantime, why not try to find where a party of Mexican miners from the old mine where ambushed somewhere along the Old Spanish Trail near the head of Spanish Fork Canyon during the 1850s. You could find a cache where Ute Indians buried several millions in gold from the Lost Mine of The Yutahs!

CHAPTER TWENTY-TWO

TRAIL'S END

We have traced the Old Spanish Trail from its earliest beginnings in Mexico to the most northern mountains and the furtherest reaches of the Great Basin. We have proven that the old trail is an ancient one, more than 400 years old. We have also shown that the legend of Cibola wasn't a western invention, but a tradition well known even before the time of Columbus. And we have travelled with nearly every conquistadore and explorer from the time of Cortez to the coming of the Mormons. The names and routes of some we know in great detail, but countless others remain unknown, with only a few "signs" to show they passed this way.

Many lost mines and missions have also been described, but so little is known of others that they have only been mentioned briefly. If nothing more, we have proven that those old places were factual and did exist, for some of them still exist and a few have been found. We have also seen evidence that Indians did not learn mining from the Spaniards, but were miners long before their arrival. And we have presented documentation that Indians were forced to work as slaves in Spanish mines.

In order to further assist those who would like to investigate the Old Spanish Trail and its lost treasures more thoroughly, an appendix follows. It contains a Spanish-English treasure dictionary of words or phrases most frequently seen in old documents, maps and waybills. It also contains an explanation of weights and measures and the various Spanish coins with their values. There is also a chronological list of expeditions made into the north along the old trail. It includes only those expeditions of record, with their probable route as closely as it can be retraced, which sometimes is only an "educated guess."

A waybill of both Spanish and Indian treasure signs and symbols has been prepared to acquaint the treasure hunter and prospector with the strange markings, signs and carvings found in the back country, and hopefully help lead the way to lost treasures of the past. It includes the most frequently encountered signs; however, there are many others peculiar to certain areas.

The author felt that the use of footnotes in the text would be distracting to the reader, therefore an extensive alphabetically arranged bibliography of information sources is attached, most of which can be found in any good library, although a few are rare or found only in selected archives. It is hoped that the reader has been given the basic information needed to seek the lost treasures of the Old Spanish Trail, the rest is up to you!

BIBLIOGRAPHY

A History Of American Mining, T.A. Rickard, McGraw-Hill, New York, 1932.

A History Of The Lost Rhoades Mines, Gale Rhoades, Dream Garden Press, Salt Lake City, Utah, 1980.

A History Of The Northern Ute People, Fred A. Conetah, Uintah-Ouray Tribe, 1982.

After Coronado, Alfred B. Thomas, University of Oklahoma, 1935.

Black Powder & Hand Steel, Otis E. Young, Jr., University of Oklahoma, 1975.

Bolton & The Spanish Borderlands, John F. Bannon, University of Oklahoma, 1964.

Conquest Of Mexico, William H. Prescott, Bostin, MA, 1843.

Conquistadors In North American History, Paul Horgan, Farrar, Straus & Co., New York, 1963.

Colorado, American Guide Series, Federal Writers Project, 1941.

Coronado, Knight Of Pueblo & Plains, Herbert E. Bolton, University of New Mexico, 1949.

De Re Metallica, Georgius Agricola, 1556.

Economic Beginnings Of The Far West, Katharine Coman, MacMillan, New York, 1925.

Forgotten Frontiers, Alfred B. Thomas, University of Oklahoma, 1932.

Forty Years Among The Indians, Daniel Jones, Westernlore Press, Salt Lake City, Utah, 1960.

History Of Hernando Cortez, Jacob Abbott, A.L. Burt & Co., New York.

History Of Nevada, Russell R. Elliott, University Of Nebraska, 1973.

History Of Utah, Hubert H. Bancroft, San Francisco, California, 1889.

Idaho, American Guide Series, Federal Writers Project, 1941.

Indian Slave Trade In The Southwest, L.R. Bailey, Westernlore Press, Los Angeles, California, 1973.

Journey Into Darkness, John Upton Terrell, William Morrow & Co., New York, 1962.

My Life Among The Savage Nations Of New Spain, Andres Perez de Ribas, Ward Ritchie Press, Los Angeles, California, 1968.

Nevada, American Guide Series, Federal Writers Project, 1941.

New Mexico, American Guide Series, Federal Writers Project, 1941.

New Spain's Far Western Frontier, David J. Weber, University of New Mexico, Albuquerque, 1979.

Old Spanish Trail, Leroy Hafen, Arthur Clark & Co., Glendale, California, 1954.

Pageant In The Wilderness, Herbert E. Bolton, Utah Historical Society, Salt Lake City, Utah, 1972.

Readings In Hispanic American History, N. Andres Cleven, Ginn & Co., Boston, MA., 1927.

Salt Lake Mining Review, Various Issues, 1899-1930, Salt Lake City, Utah.

Slavery On The Spanish Frontier, William F. Sharp, University of Oklahoma, 1976.

Spanish Institutions of the Southwest, Frank W. Blackmar, John Hopkins Press, Baltimore, Maryland, 1891.

Teodoro de Croix & The Northern Frontier Of New Spain, University of Oklahoma, 1941.

The Conquest Of New Spain, Bernal Diaz, The Folio Society, Londin, 1574.

The Conquistadors, Jean Descola, Viking Press, New York, 1957.

The Discovery Of America & The Spanish Conquest, John Fiske, Houghton Mifflin, New York, 1902.

The Dominguez-Escalante Journal, Fray Angelino Chavez, Brigham Young University Press, Provo, Utah, 1976.

The Gila, Edwin Corle, University of Nebraska, 1964.

The Golden Conquistadores, Irwin Blacker, Bobbs Merrill, Indianapolis, Indiana, 1960.

The Golden Dream, Walker Chapman, Bobbs Merrill, Indianapolis, Indiana, 1967.

The Old Trails West, Ralph Moody, Ballantine Books, New York, 1963.

The Rise Of The Spanish American Empire, Salvador de Madariaga, MacMillan, New York, 1947.

The Seven Cities Of Cibola, Stephen Clissold, Clarkston Potter Inc., New York, 1961.

The Spanish Main, Peter Woods, Time Life Books, Alexandria, Virginia, 1979.

The Spanish Traditions In America, Charles Gibson, University of South Carolina, 1968.

The Taos Trappers, David J. Weber, University of Oklahoma, 1971.

The Treasure Fleets Of The Spanish Main, Robert F. Marx, World Publishing, Cleveland, Ohio, 1968.

The Treasure Galleons, Dave Horner, Dodd Mead & Co., New York, 1971.

The Zunis Of Cibola, C. Gregory Crampton, University of Utah, 1977.

Treasure Of The Sangre de Cristos, Arthur L. Campa, University of Oklahoma, 1963.

Turquoise And Spanish Mines Of New Mexico, Staurt A. Northop, University of New Mexico, 1975.

Turquoise & The Indian, Edna Bennett, Swallow Press, Chicago, Illinois, 1966.

Utah, American Guide Series, Federal Writers Project, 1941.

Utah Historical Quarterly, Various Issues, Salt Lake City, Utah.

Western Mining, Otis E. Young, Jr., University of Oklahoma, 1970.

Wyoming, American Guide Series, Federal Writers Project, 1941.

MAJOR SPANISH EXPLORATIONS/EXPEDITIONS

1492-1503	Christopher Columbus	Caribbean, Coast of Mexico
1518	Juan de Grijalva	Coast of Mexico
1519	Hernando Cortez	Conquest of Mexico
1527	Panfilo de Narvaez	Coast of Florida
1536	Cabeza de Vaca	Florida to Arizona and Mexico
1538	Juan de Asuncion/Fray Nadal	To Arizona and Cibola
1538	Fray Marcos de Niza	Pima Villages, Cibola
1539	Melchior Diaz	Gila River, Arizona
1539	Hernando DeSoto	Gulf Coast, Mississippi Valley
1540	Hernando Coronado	North to Cibola, Quivira
1540	Hernando de Alarcon	Colorado River and Arizona
1540	Pedro de Tovar	To Tusayan, Colorado River
1540	Garcia Lopez Cardenas	Grand Canyon, Southern Utah
1565	Francisco de Ibarra	To The Land Of The Yutahs
1580	Antonio de Espejo	New Mexico and Colorado
1581	Gaspar de Sosa	Mines of New Mexico, Colorado
1585	Fray Augustin Rodriguez	Builds Mission North of New Mexico
1590	Gaspar de Sosa	Slave and Trade Expedition
1590	Luis de Carabajal	Illegal Mining in the North
1593	Juan Humana/Francisco Bonilla	Explores into Wyoming
1598	Juan de Onate	Mining in New Mexico and Colorado
1600	Marcos Farfan	Mining San Juan River Area
1604	Juan de Onate	Seeks Sierra Azul, Teguayo
1604	Fray Estevan Perea	North into Ute Country
1618	Vincent Saldivar	Mapped Teguayo
1621-1624	Fray Geronimo Salmeron	To Utah Valley, Wasatch Mountains
1628	Fray Bartolome Romero	Builds San Juan River Mission
1630	Fray Alonso Benavidas	Locates Mines At Teguayo
1640-1642	Unknown	Dates Inscribed At Glen Canyon
1650-1660	Fray Alonzo Posada	Describes Utah Valley Area
1662	Diego de Penalosa	Explores North to Platte River
1664	Juan de Archuleta	Slaving in Wyoming
1669	Alvarez de Leon	Mining in Uinta Mountains
1670	Antonio de Oterman	Make Treaty with Utes
1670s	Don Juanillo	Escapes from Utes at Utah Valley
1685	Pedro de Abalos	Mines in New Mexico
1686	Fray Alonzo De Posada	Second Trip to Utah Lake
1692	Diego de Varga	Reconquest of Ute Country
1705	Rogue De Madrid	Slaving into Colorado
1706	Juan de Uribarri	Slaving Northern Utah
1709	Juan de Uribarri	Mining in North

1713	Juan de Uribarri	Discovers Northern Mines
1719	Pedro de Villasur	Utah and Wyoming Missions
1740	Fray Carlos Delgado	Describes Northern Utah
1749	Ute-Spanish Treaty	Utah-Colorado
1756	Bernardo de Miranda	Mining Northern New Mexico
1756	Padre La Rue	Mining San Andraes Mountains
1761	Juan Maria de Rivera	Central Utah, Sevier Lake
1765	Juan Maria de Rivera	Northern Utah, Idaho
1766	Marquis de Rubi	Inspects Northern Missions
1768	Anotnio y Ramariz	Maps Teguayo, Utah Lake Area
1771	Teodoro de Croix	Inspects Northern Mines
1775	Gregorio Sandoval, Munez	Uinta Basin Mines
1776	Dominguez-Escalante	Utah Lake, Western Utah
1779	Bautistea de Anza	Slaving in Colorado
1783	Arrests Illegal Miners	Utah Area
1785-1797	Illegal Mining Parties	Utah-Colorado
1785	Philip Nolen	Americans Arrested
1786	Governor de Anza	Ute-Spanish Treaty
1792	Fray Augustin de Morfi	Northern Missions
1805	Manuel Maestes	Trading at Utah Lake
1808	Workman-Spence	Americans on Old Spanish Trail
1810-21	Father Miguel Hidalgo	Mexican Revolution
1811	Jose Rafael Sarracino	Seeks Lost Mission, Utah
1813	Mauricio Arze, Lagas Garcia	Slaving Utah Lake
1829	William Wolfskill	American Trader
1840	Father Pierre De Smet	Discovers Jesuit Mission
1844	Ute Rebellion	Utah Forts, Mines, Missions Burned, Concealed
1847	Mormon Settlement	Great Basin Americanized

SPANISH-ENGLISH TREASURE DICTIONARY

Abrevadero	watering place, trough
Alcalde	mayor, justice of the peace
Alta	high, upper
Antiqua	ancient
Arroba	weight of 25 pounds
Azoque	mercury, quicksilver
Baja	lower
Batea	wooden gold pan
Boca-Mina	tunnel portal, mine opening
Braza	measure of 65 inches
Carbonera	furnace, smelter
Carga	load, burden
Carreta	wooden wheeled cart
Casa de Moneda	mint
Castilian yard	measure of 4 hand breadths
Castellano	coin of 1/5 ounce of gold
Cavar	dig, excavate
Cerro	hill or mountain
Clerigo	clergy, clergyman
Cob, Cobo de Barra	coin, cut from a bar
Cobre	copper
Conducta	guard or convoy
Cordel	measure of 50 Castilian yards, 46.3 U.S. yards
Corregidore	magistrate
Debajo	underneath
Derrotero	diary, waybill, chart
Despablado	desert (also Desierto)
Dinero	coin, Peruvian, equal to 10¢
Distancia	distance
Doubloon	coin equal to 8 escudos
Encomienda	bill authorizing slavery
Enterrar	to bury
Escondida	hidden
Escudo	coin, a gold crown
Espanol	Spanish, Spaniard
Estado	measure, height of a man, approximately 5'4"
Estancia	ranch, hacienda
Esta Escondida	it is hidden
Este	east
Excavad	dig, excavate
Fanega	measure, 1.6 U.S. bushels
Fray, Friar	Father, Jesuit priest
Genizaro	Indian servant, trusted slave
Hallar	discover
Harqueta	fork in trail, stream
Hierro	brand, branding iron
Historia	history, historical
Hondo	deep, bottom
Ingreso	entrance, mine portal
Jornada	journey
Jornada del Muerto	journey of death
Joya	jewels
Ladrone	thief
League	measure, 5,000 paces at 32 inches, 3.45 miles prior to 1600, 2.52 miles after 1600
Linde	landmark
Llano	plain or flat land
Loma	small hill
Los Muerto no Hablen	The dead do not talk
Macho	mule
Maestre de Campo	commander, colonel
Maleta	rawhide bag
Mapa	map
Maravadi	ancient Spanish coin
Marc	coin of 8 ounces weight
Marca	mark, sign
Mas Alla	further on
Mecho	torch
Mestizo	half-breed
Mina	mine
Norte	north
Nueva Espana	New Spain

Oculto	concealed, hidden	Recondito	hidden
Oeste	west	Rico	rich
Olla	jar, kettle	Rio	river
Oro	gold		
		Secreto	secret
Padre	Father, Catholic priest	Sepultar	bury, hide
Patacon	coin, silver equal to one peso	Sierra	mountains
Perdida	lost	Sito	5,000 Castilian yards, 3 miles
Peso	monetary measure, silver	Socavor	dig under
Peso del Oro	coin of gold	Sur, Sud	south
Pichachos	peaks, mountains		
Plata	silver	Tapar	cover, hide
Ploma	lead	Tercia	measure of 5 hand spans
pozo	pit, mine shaft	Tesoro	treasure
Presidio	fortress, fortified town	Tinaja	waterhole, earthen jar
Presbitero	priest	Tiro	mine shaft
Quien Sabe	Who knows?	Vara	Spanish yard, one step of 32"
Quintal	measure of 101.43 pounds	Vara de San Ignacio	dowsing rod
Quinto	royal fifth, one-fifth	Vara de Virtud	dowsing rod
		Vasso	adobe or stone furnace
Real	group of mines	Vega	meadow
Reale	1/5 peso, 8 equal one Spanish dollar	Vena	vein of ore
		Zurron	pack sack, pouch

INDEX

Abajo Mountains, lost mine of, 92
Alarcon, Hernando, expedition and treasure, 17
American frontiersmen, French description of, 72
Anian, Straits of, legend, 3
Arrastra, descriptions, 20

Balboa, Vasco de, expedition of, 5
Bear's Ear's Trail, The, 40, 97
Becknell, William, trader, lost money cache of, 75
Benevida, Fray Alonzo, explores for mines, 31
Bonella, Francisco, builds missions in north, 25
Boren & Bether's Lost Mine, 107
Burke & Bowen's Lost Mine, 98

Cardenas, Lopez de, first explorer in Utah, 15
Cavern of Gold, Colorado, 103
Cibola, legend of, 1, 13, 19
Cobs, Spanish coins, description, 29
Colorado, Old Spanish Trail in, 38
Columbus, Christopher, voyages of, 1
Copalla, Legendary Lake of, 12, 23, 69
Coronado, Francisco, expedition of, 13
Cortez, Hernando, conquest of Mexico, 5
Crickett Hills, gold cache of, 94

De Croix, Fray Teodoro, Viceroy, 65, 71
Delgado, Fray Carlos, explores Utah area, 56
De Re Metallica, The Miner's Bible, 19
De Smet, Father Pierre, Wyoming mission and mines, 79
De Sosa, Gaspar, mining expedition, 24
De Soto, Hernando, expedition of, 17
De Vaca, Cabeza, first northern explorer, 12
Diaz, Melchior, first to seek Cibola, 13
Dip Needles, pendulums, description, 19
Dowsing, science and description of, 18

El Mina de Perdito Alma, Lost, 77
El Mina del Tiro, Lost, mining methods at, 24, 31, 44, 100
Encomienda, law allowing slavery, 9
Escalante, Fray Silvestre, expedition of, 67
Espejo, Antonio, mining, names New Mexico, 23

Farfan, Marcos, seeks northern mines, 26
Fish Lake Mountain's Lost Cache, 87
Forts: Davy Crockett, Kit Carson, Robidoux, 77

Golden Jesus, lost treasure, 74
Guzman, Gov. Nuno de, dispatches expeditions north, 12

Hoskininni, Chief, tells of Pish-La-Ki Mine, 86
House Range's Lost Spanish Mine, 92
Hoyt Peak, lost mines of, 83
Humana, Juan, lost mission treasure, 25

Ibarra, Francisco de, to Yutah country, 19
Idaho, Lost Mine on St. Mary's River, 50
Indians, cruelty to, slaves of, 10, 16, 27, 75
Indian mines and smelters, 5, 11
Indian Revolts: 1616-36, 1680-44, 1750-57, 1844, 78

Jaredite Coin Cave Cache, 82
Jaredite Mission Treasure, 52
Jesuit Map, Utah and Wyoming, 79
Jesuit Expulsion, 61
Josephine de Martinique, Lost Mine, 57, 97
Josephine, lost mine on Currant Creek, 100

La Rue, Padre, lost mine of, 58
Lawler, Frank, finds Henry Mountain Spanish mine, 99
Lincoln (Rollins Spanish) Mine, 57, 83
Lost Ashdown Brothers Mine, 87
Lost Rhoades Mine, 88
Lost Rifle Sight Mine, 92
Lost Spanish Springs Mine, Nevada, 91

Madrid, Roque, slaving expedition, 49
Maestes, Manuel, at Utah Valley, 58, 73
Merrick & Mitchell's Lost Mine, 85
Mine of Lost Souls, 77
Mining methods, Spanish, Indian, 26, 57
Mierra, Don Bernardo, map, treasure legend, 69
Mission system, Spanish, 33
Mission treasures, 45

Montezuma, Emperor, treasure of, 6, 105
Mormon gold coins, 88
Muniz, Andres & Lucrecio, mining, 62, 67

Narvaez, Panfilo, expedition of, 12
Nevada turquoise mines, 91
New Mexico, name origin, 23
New Mexico turquoise mines, 93
Niza, Fray Marcos, seeks Cibola, 73
Nolen, Philip, first American party west, 58
Noss, Dr. Milton, treasure of, 58

Onate, Juan de, expedition of, 25
Old Spanish Mines Company, 100
Old Spanish Trail, variations of, 37, 38
Otermin, Gov. Antonio, Ute Treaty, 1680 Revolt, 44

Patio Process, mining, 20
Penalosa, Gov. Diego, Maps Teguayo, 43
Perea, Fray Estevan, into Ute country 30
Pish-La-Ki, Lost Mine of Navajos, 85
Pizarro, Francisco, conquistadore, 11
Plate Fleets, 18, 55
Posades, Fray Alonzo, describes Old Spanish Trail,
    37, 47
Potosi Mine, Nevada, 91

Quivira, legend of, 16

Recapture Creek, gold bars of, 104
Rivera, Father Juan Maria, Utah Expedition of, 61
Rock Creek Mission, 50
Rodriguez, Fray Augustin, Mining Expedition of, 23
Romero, Fray Bartolome, San Juan River Mission,
    30, 34

Saldivar, Vincent, Expedition of, 30
Salmeron, Fray Geronimo, To Utah Valley, 31
San Gabriel Mission, 26
San Juan River Mission, 30, 34
San Luis Valley Mission, 47
Santa Rita Mine, 2, 73
Sarracino, Jose Rafael, Seeks Lost Settlement, 73
Sierra Azul Mine, 29, 43
Slade, Jack, Lost Cache, 80
Smith, Pegleg, Lost Placer, 76

Teguayo, Utah Valley, 15, 38, 48, 69
Tovar, Pedro, Explores Tusayan, 14
Tumacacori Mission, Lost Mines of, 62

Uinta Basin/Mountains, 44, 50, 65, 68, 77, 89
Uribarri, Juan, Captures Ute Slaves, 48
Utah, First Exploration of, 15, 31
Utah Valley, Land of Teguayo, 37, 68

Valverde's Treasure, 11
Vargas, Jose, Reconquest of the North, 47
Villasur, Pedro, Mission & Lost Treasure of, 50

Waybills, Jesuit, 52, 62, 71, 83
Wolfskill, William, Lost Ledge of Gold, 76
Wolverton, Edgar, Explorer of Henry Mountains, 40,
99
Workman & Spence, Travel Old Spanish Trail, 73
Wyoming, Lost Mission Ruins, 79

Young, Brigham, On Treasure, 81
Young, John, Lost Mine of, 83
Yutahs, Lost Mine of, 106

Catholic or Latin Cross. On travelled path or trail to mines or mission.

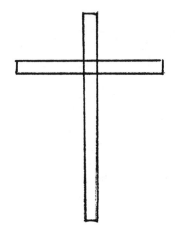

**Maltese Cross.
Found at or near mine or treasure location.**

**Mission Sign.
Near or on trail to a mission.**

**Bell.
A mission near or near mine or treasure.**

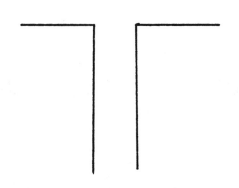

Mine Shaft.

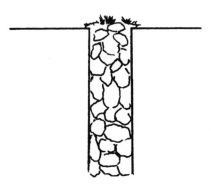

Mine shaft concealed or covered over.

Turtle.
A treasure nearby.
Also, buried possessions.

Bird.
Indicates the trail ahead crosses a marshy area.

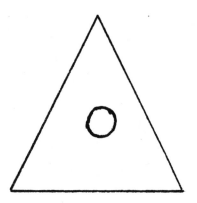

Triangle formed by trees or stones, with treasure buried at its center.

Spade or Shovel.
Treasure, dig here.

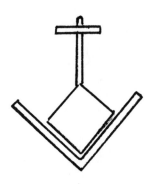

Mission and/or mines in canyon ahead.

Snake.
Travel in direction of head. If coiled, treasure is buried directly below.

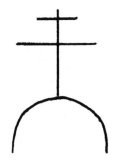

Gold.
On trail to gold mine or gold nearby.

Sign of silver.
Mine nearby or on trail to.

Azoque, mercury or quicksilver.

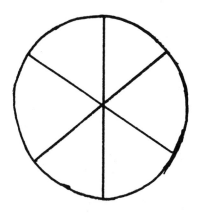

Copper, mine or something copper close or
nearby.

Mine tunnel, open.

Mine tunnel, filled in or concealed.

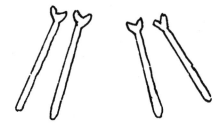

Spanish needles, each about four inches in length. Two persons keep the needles in contact. Used for seeking buried treasure.

Methods of manipulating the divining rod to find buried treasure.

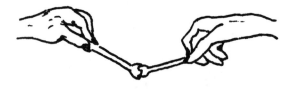

Used correctly, the needles dip or rise to indicate the direction of the treasure.

Use of the divining rod requires both practice and great dexterity.

Using the needles requires great practice to keep the needles in contact with one another.

In De Re Metallica, Agricola called the divining rod "The Enchanted Twig."